Fighting With Edge & Point

Fighting With Edge & Point

Two Guides to Use of the Broad Sword,
Small Sword, Fencing and Other Martial
Weapons & Exercises

How to Fence

Aaron A. Warford

and

A New System of Broad and Small
Sword Exercise

Thomas Stephens

LEONAUR

Fighting With Edge & Point
Two Guides to Use of the Broad Sword, Small Sword, Fencing and Other Martial
Weapons & Exercises
How to Fence
by Aaron A. Warford
and
A New System of Broad and Small Sword Exercise
by Thomas Stephens

FIRST EDITION

First published under the titles
How to Fence
and
A New System of Broad and Small Sword Exercise

Leonaur is an imprint
of Oakpast Ltd

ISBN: 978-1-78282-128-1 (hardcover)
ISBN: 978-1-78282-129-8 (softcover)

http://www.leonaur.com

Publisher's Notes

The views expressed in this book are not necessarily
those of the publisher.

Contents

How to Fence

Contents

How to Fence.

Fencing is the art of using the small-sword, or rapier. The small-sword has a straight blade, about thirty-two inches in length outside the guard, and is fashioned for *thrusting* only. Although it is an art of the greatest antiquity, very great improvements have been made in it during the last half-century, chiefly by French masters, who excel those of all other countries. This has been attributed to various causes; by some to the agility and acknowledged power of rapid physical action possessed by this nation; by others, to their natural vivacity and mental quickness. In my opinion, however, a more direct and powerful cause may be traced in the great encouragement and universal patronage which it has ever received from every grade of a chivalrous and military people.

Every regiment has its *maitre d'armes*, and every barrack its fencing-school. Indeed, in so important a light was the proper teaching of this art held, that one of the French kings (Louis XIV.) granted letters-patent to twenty eminent masters, who alone were permitted to teach in Paris. When a vacancy occurred, no interest and no favour could enable a candidate to obtain this privilege: he had to fence in public with six of these chosen masters, and if by any of them he was beaten by two distinct hits, he was considered unqualified to teach in the capital.

Independent of its value as the scientific use of the sword—the gentleman's weapon of defence, *par excellence*—fencing stands unrivalled as an *exercise*; and it is in this sense that it will now be treated. The most eminent physicians which this country have

11

produced, have all, in the most earnest manner, recommended it to the attention of the young. Thus, Dr. Clive says:

> Muscular exertion is essential in perfecting the form of the body, and those exercises which require the exercise of the greatest number of muscles are the most conducive to this end. Fencing causes more muscles to act at the same time than most other exercises. It promotes the expansion of the chest, and improves respiration, whereby the functions of the most important organs of the body are more perfectly performed.

Sir Anthony Carlisle uses similar language:

> According to my judgment, the exercise of fencing tends to promote bodily health, and the development of athletic powers. It is likewise apparent that the attitudes and exertions of fencing are conducive to the manly forms and muscular energies of the human figure.

Again, Sir Everard Home, in still stronger terms:

> Of all the different modes in which the body can be exercised, there is none, in my judgment, that is capable of giving strength and velocity, as well as precision, to the action of all the voluntary muscles of the body in an equal degree as the practice of fencing, and none more conducive to bodily health.

I shall give one more extract from another physician of equal eminence, Dr. Babbington:

> I am of opinion that, in addition to the amusement which this exercise (fencing) affords, it is particularly calculated to excite in young persons a greater degree of energy and circumspection than they might otherwise possess; and it is obvious that, in respect of health, that mode of exertion is *superior to all others*, which, while it gives motion and activity to every part of the body, produces at the same time corresponding interest in the mind.

Sir John Sinclair, Dr. Pemberton, &c., speak in terms equally recommendatory.

To avoid all danger in the lessons and practice, foils are substituted for real swords. Strong wire masks are worn on the face, a well-padded glove on the hand; and the upper part of the body, at which alone the thrusts are aimed, is protected by a strong jacket, the right side and collar of which should be of leather.

The first movement a beginner has to learn, is the manner of placing himself in the position called

THE GUARD.

It is from this position that all movements are made, whether offensive or defensive. Let the beginner be placed with his knees straight, his feet at right angles, heel to heel; the right foot, right side, and face directed to the master. The body must be held upright and firm, the arms hanging down by the side, but easily and without constraint, the left hand holding the foil a few inches beneath its guard. Next, let him bring the right hand across the body, and seize the foil-handle; by a second movement, bring the foil above the head, the hands separating as they ascend, until both arms be nearly extended upwards and outwards. Here pause. This may be called the *first position* of the Guard.

These movements should be frequently practiced, as they accustom the arms to move independently of the body, flatten the joints of the shoulders, and give prominence to the chest.

To arrive at the *second position* of the Guard, the right arm, with the foil, is brought down to the front, until the right elbow is a little above and in advance of the waist; the fore-arm and foil sloping upwards; the point of the foil being the height of the upper part of the face; then, by a second movement, the learner must sink down, separating the knees, and stepping forward with the right foot fourteen or sixteen inches; for, of course, the guard of a tall man will be wider than that of a short one. However, his own comfort in the position will direct him as to the distance; and the general rule is, that the knee of the left leg will jut over the toes of the left foot, and the right leg from ankle to knee be

THE ADVANCE

perpendicular. It is in this position that he will receive all attacks from an adversary, and from this position will all his own attacks be made. Also in this position will he advance upon an adversary, when beyond hitting distance. The step in the advance is usually about that of the width of the Guard, although of course this would vary with circumstances. The step is made by advancing the right foot the distance I have named; and on its reaching the ground, the left foot is brought up, and takes its place. To Retreat, the reverse of the above movement is made. The left foot takes the lead, stepping to the rear about as far as the right had stepped to the front; the right occupying its place on its taking up its new position.

The next movement, the Longe, is a very important movement, and is rather difficult to make properly, and fatiguing to practice. Indeed, the first movements in fencing are the most trying to the learner; and he must not be discouraged if he fails to do them correctly at first—practice only will give him this power. The Longe is that extension of body which accompanies every attack, and is thus made:—The right arm is extended straight from the shoulder, the arm and blade being on the same level; by a second movement, the right foot is raised from the ground, and a step made forward, about eighteen inches in length, while the left remains firmly planted in its place. At the instant that this step is made, the left hand is allowed to fall within a few inches of the left thigh, and the left knee is stiffened back until the leg is perfectly straight.

The thigh of the right leg will now be in a position nearly horizontal; from the knee downwards perpendicular. Having executed the Longe, the next movement to be made is the Recover; that is, to return from the position of the Longe to that of the Guard, and is thus effected:—The left arm is nimbly thrown up to its place, the right arm drawn in, and the left knee re-bent. These movements must be made at the same time, as it is their *united* action that enables a person to recover from so extended a position as the Longe quick enough to avoid a thrust if his own attack has failed.

The Longe,

These movements must be frequently practiced before any others are attempted—the Guard, the Advance, the Retreat, the Longe, and the Recover; and when the learner has attained some proficiency in them, he may begin the more delicate movements of attack and defence. Of these I will now speak.

THE ENGAGE.

It is customary for adversaries, on coming to the Guard, to *Engage*, or to join blades, on what is called the *inside*, that is, the *right* side; although there are occasions on which it is advisable to engage on the *outside*, or on the left; otherwise called the *Quarte* or *Tierce* sides.

Two men thus opposed to each other will at once perceive that there are two lines of attack open to them, *i. e.* the line inside and the line outside the blade—these, and no more. But these may be, and in fencing are, subdivided into inside above the hand, and inside under the hand, and the same subdivision for outside. This gives four lines of attack—or, to speak more simply, gives four openings through which an adversary may be assailed. Now, to protect each of these assailable points, are four defensive movements, called Parades.

Each opening has its own parade or defence, and each parade will guard its own opening, and, strictly speaking, no other. The opening inside above the hand is defended by two parades.

As its name imports, the first and most natural parade is that of *Prime*. The action of drawing the sword from its sheath is almost exactly the movement made use of in the parade of Prime.

In this parade the hand is raised as high as the forehead, so that the fencer can see his opponent's face under his wrist. The blade of the foil is almost horizontal, but the point is rather lowered towards the ground. As this parade will throw the right side of the body open to the adversary's sword, it is good play to disengage from left to right, and deliver a rapid thrust at the adversary, in order to anticipate him before he can bring his own sword round for another thrust. His point will be thrown far out

THE ENGAGE.

of line, so that he is behind-hand in point of time.

This is a very useful parade for fencers of short stature, as they can sometimes get in their blade under their adversary's arm, after they have parried his thrust.

The other parade is that of Quarte.

It is thus formed. On the approach of the point of an adversary's blade (and how these approaches are made I will presently explain), the right hand is moved a few inches—three or four will be enough—across the body on the inside, the hand being neither depressed nor raised, and the foil being kept on the same slope as in the Guard. This guards the body on the inside above the hand, but (and here comes an important law in fencing) the very movement which has guarded the body on one side has exposed it on the other; this is the case with all the simple parades.

Suppose, now, that the exposed part *outside above* the hand were assailed, then the defence for it is the parade of Tierce.

It is formed by turning the hand with the nails downwards, and crossing to the opposite side some six or eight inches, the hand and point at the same elevation as before; this will guard this opening. If, however, the attack has been made *under* instead of over the hand, then the proper parade would have been *seconde*.

There is another method of parade called *quarte* over the arm—which is executed by making about the same parade as in Tierce, with this exception—first, the hand is retained in its original position, with the nails upwards, and secondly, the point is not raised over the eye of the adversary.

It is rather more delicate than Tierce, but wants its power and energy. The ripostes, or reply thrusts, are made as they would have been had the parade been that of Tierce.

Seconde is formed by turning the hand in the same position in which it was turned for tierce, but the point of the foil slopes as much downwards as in tierce it did upwards; the direction and distance for the hand to traverse being the same. Again, had the attack been delivered at none of these, but at the *inside*

QUARTE.

Tierce

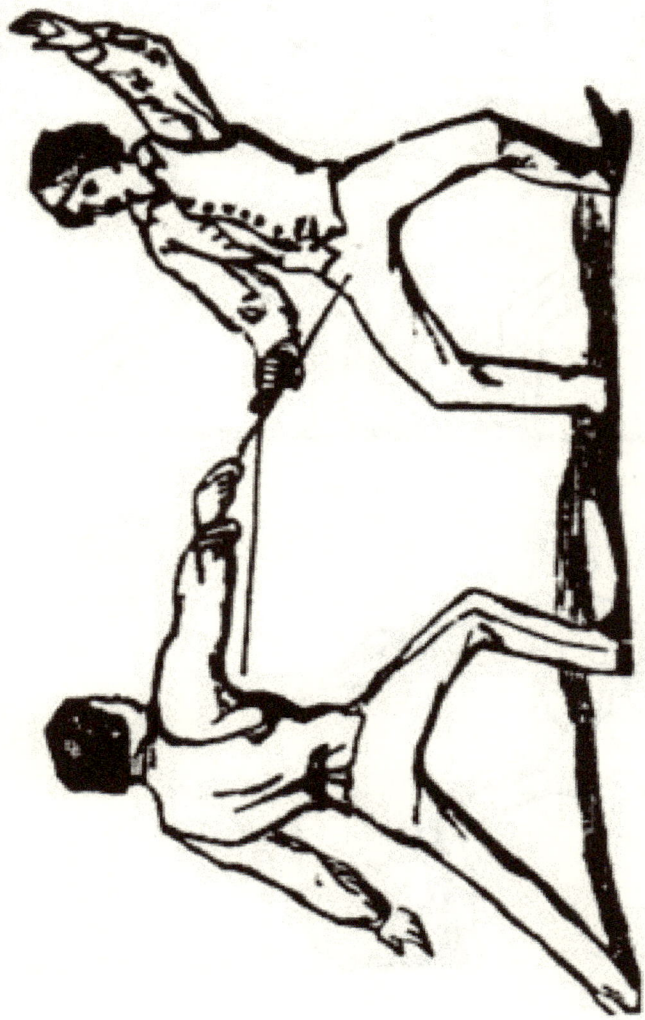

QUARTE OVER THE ARM

under the hand, then the proper parade would have been Demi-Cercle, which, as its name expresses, is a half-circle, described by a sweep of the blade traversing the *under* line. Next comes the parade of Octave.

In this parade the hand is held as in Quarte; the hilt of the foil is kept lower than that of the opponent: the blade is almost horizontal, the point being only slightly lower than the hilt, and directed towards the body of the adversary.

Octave is extremely useful when the fencer misses his parade of *Demi-cercle,* as there is but a short distance for the point to traverse, and it generally meets the blade of the adversary before the point can be properly fixed. Moreover, it brings the point so near the adversary's body, that he will not venture to make another thrust until he has removed the foil.

Thus I have enumerated, and partly explained, the forms and uses of these four parades: they are called Simple Parades, to distinguish them from another set of defensive movements, called *Contre*-Parades.

I have said and shown that a man standing foil in hand, in the position of the guard, is exposed in four distinct places to thrusts from an adversary within longeing distance. I have also shown that he has a defence for each of these exposed places; but if a man has but *one* defence for each assailable part, then his adversary, knowing beforehand what the defence must be, would be prepared beforehand to deceive him. But if he has a reserve—if he has a *second* defence for each part—then the adversary cannot tell what the defence will be, until his attack, false or real, is begun.

To meet this contingency, a second series of defences have been devised, which are of an entirely different nature from the *Simple* Parades.

Again, as each of the simple parades is framed to guard only one opening, it was found desirable that the *contre*-parades should be of a more comprehensive character. They are therefore devised so that each is capable of protecting the entire front. It is evident that this object could not be attained without the

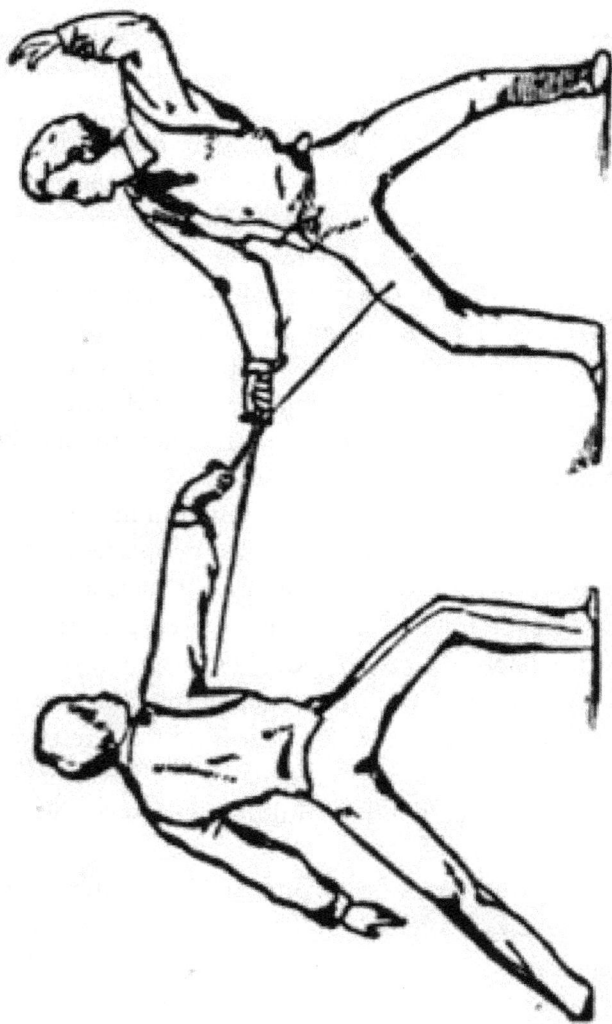

OCTAVE

sacrifice of quickness, because a larger space must be traversed, and therefore more time is occupied with a contre than a simple parade.

To know one *contre*-parade is virtually to know all, as they are all formed on the same plan. They are all full circles in the position of hand and direction of foil of the different simple parades; or more clearly speaking, each simple parade has a *contre*-parade; there are, therefore, four simple and four *contre*-parades, which may be thus arranged:

Quart	*Contre de Quarte*
Tierce	*Contre de Tierce*
Seconde	*Contre de seconde*
Demi-cercle	*Contre de Cercle*

I have said that a *contre*-parade is a full circle in the position of hand and direction of blade of its simple; thus, *contre de quarte* is made by retaining the hand in the position of *quarte*, while the foil describes a circle descending on the inside, and returning by the outside to the place of its departure. So with all the others, the foil *following the direction of the simple* parade, of which it is the *contre*. These complete the entire system of defences.

I now come to the movements of an opposite nature, namely, the Attacks, and shall begin with the most simple of them. I will again suppose two adversaries standing *en guard*, within longeing distance of each other: now the most simple movement that the attacking party could make would be the Straight Thrust to the outside or inside, according to his line of engagement. I have, in describing the longe, in effect described the straight thrust; it is but a longe in a straight line, taking care, however, to feel firmly the adversary's blade, but taking care also not to press or lean on it during the delivering of the thrust.

Next in character comes the Disengagement.

This attack is made by dropping the point of the foil beneath the adversary's blade, and raising it on the opposite side, at the same time, rising with the arm fully extended; on the completion of the extension the longe is made and the thrust delivered.

The One-Two is but a double disengagement, the first being but a feint or false attack, to induce the adversary to form a parade to cover the part threatened, for the covering of one part of the body exposes the opposite; the second disengagement is made to take advantage of this exposure. The arm is extended half-way on the first, and then wholly on the second, to be immediately followed by the longe.

The Beat and Thrust.

This is another variety of attack. Supposing the adversary's blade to be firmly joined to yours, when you wished to deliver a *straight thrust*, there would then be danger of your falling upon his point. This danger is avoided by giving a slight beat on his blade the instant preceding your extension of arm, of course to be followed *en suite* by the longe.

The companion attack to this one is the Beat and Disengagement.

The *beat* here takes the character of the first disengagement in *one-two*, *i. e.* becomes a *feint*, and is intended to induce the adversary to return to the place he occupied when the beat was made. You then immediately pass to the opposite side of his blade in the manner described in the *disengagement*.

It will be seen that all these movements pass *under* the adversary's blade. However, there are certain situations in the *assault*, as a fencing about is called, when an adversary is more assailable *over the point* than under the blade; for this purpose there is what the French call the *coupe sur peint*, or Cut Over the Point.

It is thus made:—By the action of the hand, and without drawing it back at all, the foil is raised and brought down on the opposite side of the adversary's blade, the arm being extended during its fall to the horizontal position, on attaining which the longe is delivered.

Cut Over and Disengagement is on the same principal as the *one-two* and the *beat and disengagement*. On the adversary opposing the first movement (the cut) with a parade, the second movement (the disengagement) is made to the opposite side, to be followed, of course, by the longe, the extension of the arm being divided between the two movements.

These attacks are called simple attacks, because they may be parried by one or more simple parades, according to the number of movements in the attack. In fact, every attack can be parried, and every parade can be deceived; it is the *additional* movement last made which hits or guards.

Thus, you threaten by a disengagement to the outside; your adversary bars your way effectually by the parade of *tierce*; you make a second disengagement to the inside, which is now exposed from the very fact of the outside being guarded (for both lines of attack cannot be guarded at the same time), thus converting your attack into *one-two*; but if your adversary parries *quarte* on your *second* movement, your attack would be warded off. This can be carried much further, but the above will, I think, be sufficient to explain the nature of simple parades and attacks.

To deceive a *contre*-parade, a separate movement, called a Double,

has been invented; it is very simple in principle, and admirably answers the purpose. For instance if you were to threaten your adversary by a disengagement to the outside, and if, instead of tierce, he parried *contra de quarte*, the double is then made by your making a *second* disengagement *to the same side as the first*, for it will be found that his *contra de quarte* has replaced the blade in the positions they occupied previous to your disengagement. You will then have an opening, and may finish the attack by the longe.

As all the contra-parades are on the same plan and principle, so are all the doubles. Of course, it is understood that you will make all the movements of the double *en suite*, and without allowing your adversary's blade to overtake yours.

ALL FEINTS.

The foregoing movements having been well practiced in the lesson, the next step is that of *all feints* and *all parades*, and may be practiced either with a master or fellow-pupil. The practice consists of one pupil standing on the defensive *entirely*, while another assumes the offensive, and attacks him with *all* the *feints* of which he is master, the other, of course, defending with all his parades. It is excellent practice, as it accustoms the pupil to think for himself gradually, he having thus but one set of movements to think about. He is therefore enabled to make them boldly, without having to encounter unknown movements from his adversary.

It also enables him to see the extent of his resources, both for attack and defence. When he can both attack and defend with some presence of mind, he may then begin the Assault; that is, he may encounter an adversary, to attack or defend as occasion presents. He is then left to his own resources entirely. The following General Advice, given by a very eminent fencer and excellent teacher, cannot fail to be of use:

> Do not put yourself on the position of the guard within the reach of your adversary's thrusts, especially at the time of drawing your sword.
> If you are much inferior, make no long assaults.
> Do nothing that is useless; every movement should tend to your advantage.
> Let your movements be made as much within the line of your adversary's body as possible.
> Endeavour both to discover your adversary's designs and to conceal your own.
> Two skilful men, acting together, fight more with their heads than their hands.
> The smaller you can make the movements with your foil, the quicker will your point arrive at your adversary's body.
> Do not endeavour to give many thrusts on the longe, thus running the risk of receiving one in the interim.
> If your adversary drops his foil by accident, or in consequence of a smart parade of yours, you should immediately pick it up, and present it to him politely.
> Always join blades (if possible) previously to another attack, after a hit is given.

Broadsword Exercise

The principal distinction between the broadsword and the rapier is, that the latter is formed only for thrusting, while the former is adapted for cutting also. Indeed, those who use the broadsword are, in my opinion, too apt to neglect the use of the point, and to give their attention almost exclusively to the cuts.

The first lesson in the sword exercise is necessarily to know how to stand. The learner should be instructed to perform the different movements by word of command, remembering to consider the first parts of the word as a caution, and not to stir until the *last* syllable is uttered. At the last syllable, the movement should be performed smartly. In giving the word, the instructor always makes a slight pause, in order to give his pupils time to remember what they must do. For example, the words Draw Swords is given thus, Draw . . . Swords—the word swords being spoken smartly, in order that the movement may correspond.

Positions.

First Position.—Make the target (For target, see page 28) about fourteen inches in diameter, and place it on the wall, having its centre about four feet from the ground. Draw a perpendicular line from the spot at the bottom of the target to the ground, and continue it on the floor, in order to insure the proper position of the heels. The learner stands perfectly upright opposite the target, with his right side towards it, his heels close together, his right toe pointing to the target, and his left foot at right angles with the left. His arms must be clasped behind his back, his right palm supporting the left elbow, and his left hand

Fig. 1

Fig. 2

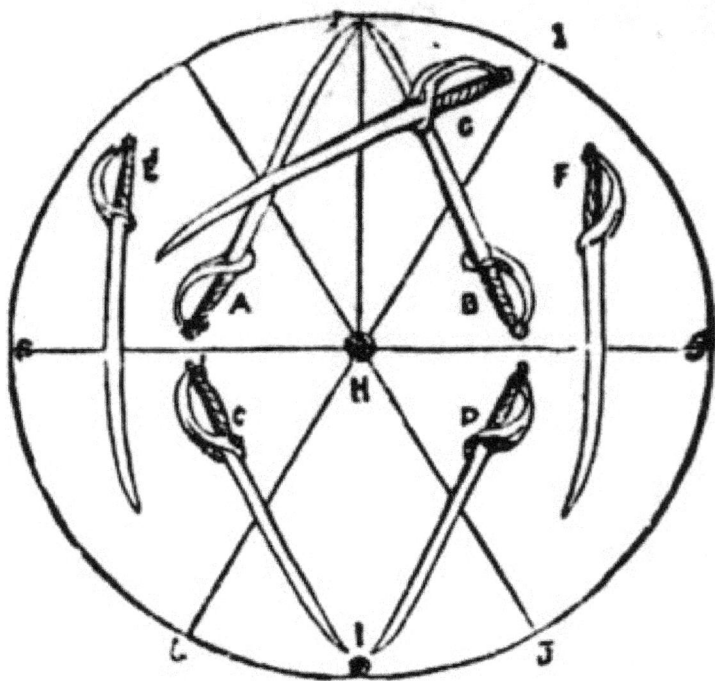

Target.

grasping the right arm just above the elbow. In this position, he must bend both knees and sink down as far as possible. This will not be very far at first, but he will soon sink down quite easily.

Second Position.—This is accomplished by placing the right foot smartly in front, about sixteen or fourteen inches before the left. (See fig. 1.) He must accustom himself to balance himself so perfectly on his left foot that he can place the right either before or behind it, without losing his balance.

Third Position.—The third position must then be learned. This consists of stepping well forward with the right foot, until the left knee is quite straight, and the right knee exactly perpendicularly placed over the right foot. Great care must be taken to keep the heels exactly in the same line and the body perfectly upright. (See fig. 2.)

These preliminaries having been settled, the learner stands upright before the target. A sword is then put into his hand, and the target is explained as follows:—

TARGET.

The interior lines represent the cuts. Cut one being directed from No. 1 diagonally through the target, coming out at 4. Cut two is the same, only from left to right. Three is made upwards diagonally, and four is the same, only in the opposite direction. Cut five is horizontally through the target from right to left, and six from left to right. Cut seven is perpendicularly downwards. Care must be taken that the cuts are fairly given with the edge.

The swords drawn on the target represent the guards. The seventh guard ought, however, not to be made directly across, but must have the point directly rather forwards and downwards, as a cut 7 glides off the blade, and can be instantly answered either by a thrust or by cut 1.

The two dark circles represent the places where the thrusts take effect.

The learner begins by taking the sword in his right hand, having its edge toward the target and its back resting on his shoulder. His right arm is bent at right angles, and the elbow against his side. The left hand must rest upon the hip, the thumb being to the rear. At the word—Cuts and Guards.

CUTS.

Cut 1.—The young swordsman extends his right arm, and makes the cut clear through the target. When the point has cleared the target, continue the sweep of the sword, and by the turn of the wrist bring it with its back on the left shoulder, its edge towards the left. The arm is then ready for

Cut 2.—Bring the sword from 2 to 3, continue the movement of the sword, and turn the wrist so that the point is below the right hip and the edge towards the ground.

Cut 3.—Cut through the target diagonally, bringing the sword from No. 3 to No. 2, and bring the sword onwards, so that it rests with the edge downwards, and point below the left hip. At first point.

Cut 4.—Cut from 4 to 1, and bring the sword round until its point is over the right shoulder, and its edge well to the right.

Cut 5.—At the word Five, make a horizontal cut from 5 to 6, and sweep the sword round until it rests on the left shoulder, with its edge to the left, and its point well over the shoulder.

Cut 6.—Cut horizontally through the target from 6 to 5, and bring the sword over the head with the edge upwards, and its point hanging over the back. From this position,—

Cut 7.—Make a downward stroke until the sword reaches the centre of the target. Arrest it there, and remain with the arm extended, waiting for the word.

POINTS.

First Point.—Draw back the sword, until the right wrist is against the right temple, the edge of the sword being upwards. Make a slight pause, and then thrust smartly forward toward the centre of the target, raising the right wrist as high as No. 1, and pressing the left shoulder well back.

Second Point.—Turn the wrist round to the left, so that the edge comes upwards, draw the hand back until it rests on the breast, and give the point forwards, to the centre of the target, raising the hand as before.

Third Point.—Give the handle of the sword a slight twist in the hand to the right, so that the edge again comes uppermost, and the guard rests against the back of the hand. Draw back the hand until it rests against the right hip, and deliver it forward towards the spot at the bottom of the target, raising the wrist as high as the spot in the centre. The object in raising the wrist is to deceive the eye of the opponent, who will be more likely to notice the position of your wrist than of your point. In all the thrusts, the left shoulder should be rather brought forward before the point is given, and pressed well back while it is being delivered.

FIRST POINT

Second Point

THIRD POINT

GUARDS.

Wait after the third point has been delivered for the word, Defend.—At this word draw up the hand smartly, and form the first guard. Make the other guards in succession as they are named, while the instructor proves their accuracy by giving the corresponding cuts. The guards must be learned from the target, by placing the sword in exactly the same position as those delineated. The guards are these:

A First guard
B Second
C Third.
D Fourth
E Fifth
F Sixth
G Seventh.

The two spots H and I mark the places towards which the points are made, H for the first and second point, I for the third.

PARRY.

The parry or parade of a thrust is executed with the back of the sword. The firmest way of parrying is to hold the sword perpendicular, with its edge to the right and its hilt about the height of and close to the right shoulder; then, by sweeping the sword round from left to right, any thrust within its sweep is thrown wide of the body.

The parry is executed with the wrist, and not with the arm, which must not move.

HANGING GUARD.

When the pupil is acquainted with both cuts and guards, he should learn the hanging guard, a most useful position, as it keeps the body well hidden under the sword, and at the same time leaves the sword in a good position to strike or thrust.

It is accomplished in the following way:—Step out to the second position, raise the arm until the hand is just over the

HANGING GUARD

right foot, and as high as the head. The edge of the sword is upwards, and the point is directed downwards and towards the left. The left shoulder is pressed rather forward, and the neck and chest drawn inward.

In this position, the swordsman is in a position to receive or make an attack as he may think fit. It is rather fatiguing at first, owing to the unaccustomed position of the arm and head, but the fatigue is soon overcome, and then it will be found that there is no attitude which gives equal advantages.

There are two other modes of standing on guard, each possessing their peculiar advantages. These are, the inside and outside guard. The inside guard is made as follows:

INSIDE GUARD.

Stand in the second position, having the wrist of the right hand nearly as low as the waist, the hand being exactly over the right foot. The point of the sword is raised as high as the eyes, and the edge is turned inwards.

OUTSIDE GUARD.

The outside guard is formed in the same manner as the inside, with the exception that the edge of the sword is turned well outwards.

To get to the hanging guard, the words are given as follows:—
Inside guard—outside guard—guard.

ATTACK AND DEFENCE.

The swordsman having learned thus far, is taught to combine the three movements of striking, thrusting, and guarding, by the following exercise:—

1. Inside Guard.
2. Outside Guard.
3. Guard.
4. Cut One.
5. First Guard.
6. Cut Two.
7. Second Guard.

8. Cut Three.

9. Third Guard.

10. Cut Four.

11. Fourth Guard.

12. Cut Five.

13. Fifth Guard.

14. Cut Six.

15. Sixth Guard.

16. Cut Seven.

17. Seventh Guard.

18. First Point. [Prepare for the point in First Position.] Two. [Thrust in Third Position.]

19. Second Point. [Prepare for it in First Position.] Two. [Thrust in Third Position.]

20. Third Point. [Prepare.] Two. [Thrust.]

21. Parry. [Prepare to parry in First Position.] Two. [Parry.]

22. Guard.

The young swordsman must remember that in this, as in all the exercises, the cuts and points must be given in the third position, as in the accompanying illustration, which shows the swordsman just as he has delivered the seventh cut, and is waiting for the next word before he resumes the first position.

The guards, on the contrary, are given in the first position, as is seen in the figure on page 40, which illustrates the seventh guard.

These exercises are always learned with the single-stick, or basket-hilted cudgel, in order to avoid the dangers which would be inevitable if the sword were used. But as the single-stick is only an imitation of the sword, I will give the method of getting the sword out of the sheath into any position required.

DRAW SWORDS.

The first word of command is *draw swords.* At the word *draw,* seize the sheath just below the hilt, with the left hand, and raise the hilt as high as the hip, at the same time grasping the hilt with the right hand, turning the edge of the sword to the rear, and

SEVENTH CUT.

Seventh Guard.

drawing it partially from the sheath, to insure its easy removal.

At the word *swords*, draw the blade smartly out of the scabbard, throwing the point upwards, at the full extent of the arm, the edge being still to the rear.

RECOVER SWORDS.

The wrist is now smartly lowered until it is level with the chin, the blade upright, and the edge to the left. This is the position of recover swords. The elbow must be kept close to the body as in the cut.

CARRY SWORDS.

The wrist is now sharply lowered until the arm hangs at its full length, the wrist being in the line with the hip, the edge of the sword to the front, and its back resting in the hollow of the shoulder, the fingers lightly holding the hilt. The left hand hangs at the side until the word *inside guard*, when it is placed on the left hip.

SLOPE SWORDS.

At the word *swords*, raise the right hand smartly, until it forms a right angle at the elbow.

RETURN SWORDS.

At the word, raise the blade until it is perpendicular, move the hilt to the hollow of the left shoulder, drop the point of the sword into the scabbard (which has been grasped by the left hand and slightly raised), at the same time turning the edge to the rear. Pause an instant, and send the sword smartly into the sheath, removing both hands as the hilt strikes against the mouth of the scabbard; drop them to the side, with the palms outwards, and in the first position.

PRACTICES.

There are many exercises with the broadsword, called *practices*. I have given one of them, which is to be practiced alone; but when the pupil has attained some confidence in the use of his weapon, he must be placed opposite another pupil, and they

RECOVER SWORDS.

must go through them, each taking the attack and defence in turn.

The young swordsman must be provided with a very stout wire mask, which defends the face and part of the neck, and which should be worked in a kind of helmet above, to guard against the disastrous consequences of receiving the seventh guard. No practices, loose or otherwise, should be permitted without the masks, as neither party would be able to cut or thrust with proper confidence.

SECOND PRACTICE.

This is very useful in teaching the point and parry, as well as giving steadiness on the feet. Two boys are placed opposite each other, at just such a distance, that when perfectly erect they can touch the hilt of their adversary's sword with the point of their own.

The one who gives the first point is called Front Rank (there may be a dozen in each rank, each having tried the distance to his right by extending his sword), and the one who gives first parry is called Rear Rank.

Word of Command.	Front Rank.	Rear Rank.
Guard	Hanging guard	Hanging guard
Third point	Prepare to give third point	Prepare to parry
Point	{Give third point,} {and when parried} {spring back to the} {first position, and} {prepare to parry}	Parry third point, and prepare to give third point
Point	{Parry third point,} { and prepare for} {third point}	Give third point, and prepare to parry

Point, &c. &c.

This should be continued until both are weary.

Both swordsmen should learn to do it more rapidly every time they practice. Next time of going through it, front rank and rear rank change places, as they must do in all the practices.

THIRD PRACTICE.

Word of Command.	Front Rank.	Rear Rank.
Guard	Hanging guard	Hanging guard
Leg	Cut four	Cut seven
Inside guard	Inside guard	Inside guard
Leg	Cut six [at leg]	Cut six [at neck]
Outside guard	Outside guard	Outside guard
Leg	Cut five [at leg]	Cut five [at neck]
Guard	Hanging guard	Hanging guard
Slope Swords	Slope swords	Slope swords

In this and the other practices the cuts must be delivered in the third position, and the guards in the first. In the third and fourth practices the cuts must be given lightly, as many of them are not intended to be guarded, but merely to show the powers of the sword in various positions.

FOURTH PRACTICE.

Word of Command.	Front Rank.	Rear Rank.
Guard	Hanging guard	Hanging guard
Head	Seventh cut	Seventh guard
Head	Seventh guard	Cut seven
Leg	Fourth cut	Seventh guard
Leg	Seventh guard	Fourth cut
Head	Seventh cut	Seventh guard
Head	Seventh guard	Seventh cut
Guard	Hanging guard	Hanging guard
Slope swords	Slope swords	Slope swords

In this and the preceding exercise, the power of shifting the leg is shown. If two swordsmen attack each other, and No. 1 strikes at the leg of No. 2, it will be better for No. 2 not to oppose the cut by the third or fourth guard, but to draw back the leg smartly, and cut six or seven at the adversary's head or neck.

In loose play, as it is called, *i. e.*, when two parties engage with swords without following any word of command, but strike and guard as they can, both players stand in the second position, because they can either advance or retreat as they choose, and can longe out to the third position for a thrust or a cut, or spring up to the first position for a guard with equal ease.

It is often a kind of trap, to put the right leg more forward than usual, in order to induce the adversary to make a cut at it. When he does so, the leg is drawn back, the stroke passes harmless, and the deceived striker gets the stick of his opponent on his head or shoulders.

We now come to a very complicated exercise, called the Fifth Practice.

FIFTH PRACTICE.

Word of Command.	Front Rank.	Rear Rank.
Draw swords	Draw swords	Draw swords
Inside guard	Inside guard	Inside guard
Outside guard	Outside guard	Outside guard
Guard	Hanging guard	Hanging guard
Head	Seventh cut	Seventh guard
Head	Seventh guard	Seventh cut
Arm	Second cut [at arm]	Second guard
Head	Seventh guard	Seventh cut
Head	Seventh cut	Seventh guard
Arm	Second guard	Second cut [at arm]
Head	Seventh cut	Seventh guard
Head	Seventh guard	Seventh cut
Right side	Sixth cut	Sixth guard
Head	Seventh guard	Seventh cut
Head	Seventh cut	Seventh guard
Right side	Sixth guard	Sixth cut
Guard	Hanging guard	Hanging guard

This practice is capital exercise, and looks very imposing. All these practices ought to be so familiar that the words of command are not needed, the only word required being First, Second, or Third practices, as the case may be.

I can remember once, that two of my pupils had attained such a mastery of their weapons that we used often to go through the practice with real swords. On one occasion, we were acting a charade, and my eldest pupil and myself were enacting the part of two distinguished foreigners (country unknown) who were to get up a fight. So we began by a little quarrel, and finally drew our swords and set hard to work at the fifth practice, which we could do with extreme rapidity, and without the use of words of command. The spectators were horrified, and the ladies greatly alarmed; for there seems to be no particular order in that practice, and an inexperienced eye would certainly fancy that the combatants were in earnest.

FORT AND FEEBLE.

The half of the sword-blade next the hilt is called the "fort," because it is the strongest place on which the cut of an adversary can be received. Always parry and guard with the fort of your sword, as, if you try to guard a cut with the "feeble," which is the remaining half of the blade, your guard will be forced, and the cut take effect.

DRAWING CUT.

The drawing cut is made best with a curved sword, and is executed by placing the edge of the sword on the object, and drawing it over it until it is severed. A good large mangel-wurzel is capital practice. Place the root loose on a table, stand at arm's-length from it, lay the edge of the sword lightly on it, and slice the root by repeatedly drawing the sword over it. This is very difficult, although it looks easy enough, and is sure to jar the arm from the wrist to the shoulder the first time or two, while the sword glides off as if the root were cased in polished steel. However, a little practice will soon overcome the difficulty. This cut is much in use among the Sikhs.

Never look at your own sword, but watch the eye and sword-wrist of your opponent.

Remember that the great point in this exercise, as in fencing, is to gain time. Endeavour, therefore, to advance your point nearer your adversary than his is to you.

Begin the assault out of distance, so that neither party can complain of being taken by surprise.

If the two parties exchange a cut or a thrust at the same moment, the one who gave his cut or thrust in the third position is victorious.

When a cut or thrust is made, the one who receives it passes his sword, *i. e.*, stick, into his left hand, and his opponent comes to inside guard.

Always spring back to the second position after delivering a cut or thrust.

Keep the line of direction carefully, or you will leave an open space for the adversary to get his sword into.

Last and most important,—Don't lose your temper!

Archery

For the purposes of the archer the following implements are required, which may be obtained at any of the principal makers in New York or Boston—first, the bow; secondly, the arrow; thirdly, a quiver, pouch, and belt; fourthly, a tassel and grease-pot; fifthly, an arm-guard or brace, and a shooting glove; sixthly, a target or targets; and seventhly, a scoring card.

The bow is the most important article in archery, and also the most expensive. It is usually from five to six feet in length, made of a single piece of yew, or of lancewood and hickory glued together back to back. The former suits gentlemen the best, and the latter being more lively is better adapted for the short, sharp pull of the ladies. The wood is gradually tapered, and at each end is a tip of horn, the one from the upper end being longer than the other or lower one. The strength of bows is marked in pounds, varying from 25 to 80 lbs. Ladies' bows are from 25 to 40 lbs. in strength, and those of gentlemen from 50 to 80 lbs. One side of the bow is flat, called its "back;" the other rounded, is called the "belly;" and nearly in the middle, where the hand should take the hold, it is lapped round with velvet, and that part is called the "handle." In each of the tips of horn is a notch for the string called "the nock."

Bowstrings are made of hemp or flax, the former being the better material; for though at first they stretch more, yet they wear longer, and stand a harder pull as well as being more elastic in the shooting. In applying a fresh string to a bow, be careful in opening it not to break the composition that is on it; cut the tie, take hold of the eye, which will be found ready-worked at one end, let the other part hang down, and pass the eye over the upper end of the bow. If for a lady, it may be held from 2 to 2½ inches below the nock; if for a gentleman, half an inch lower, varying it according to the length and strength of the bow; then run your hand along the side of the bow and string to the bottom nock, turn it round that and fix it by the noose, called the "timber noose," taking care not to untwist the string in making it. This noose is merely a simple turn back and twist without a knot, but it is better seen than described.

When strung, a lady's bow will have the string about 5 or 5½ inches from the belly; and a gentleman's about half an inch more. The part opposite the handle, is bound round with waxed silk, in order to prevent its being frayed by the arrow. As soon as a string becomes too soft and the fibres too straight, rub it with bees-wax, and give it a few turns in the proper direction, so as to shorten it and twist its strands a little tighter; a spare string should always be provided by the shooter.

The arrows are differently shaped by the various makers; some being of uniform thickness throughout, while others are protuberant in the middle; some, again, are larger at the point than at the feather end, which I believe to be the best form for shooting; and others are quite the reverse. They are now invariably made of white deal, with points of iron or brass riveted on, but generally having a piece of heavy wood spliced on to the deal between it and the point, by which their flight is improved.

At the other end a piece of horn is inserted, in which is a notch for the string; and they are armed with three feathers glued on, one of which is of a different colour to the others, and is intended to mark the proper position of the arrow when placed on the string—this one always pointing from the bow. These feathers, properly applied, give a rotary motion to the arrow which causes its flight to be straight. They are generally from the wing of the turkey or goose. The length and weight vary; the latter being marked in sterling silver coin, stamped on the arrow in plain figures. It is usual to paint a crest, or a distinguishing ring or rings, on the arrow just above the feathers, by which they may be known in shooting at the target.

The quiver is merely a tin case painted green, and is intended for the security of the arrows when not in use. The pouch and belt are worn round the waist, and the latter contains those arrows which are actually being shot.

A pot to hold grease for touching the glove and string, and a tassel to wipe the arrows, are hung to the belt. The grease is composed of deer-suet, or of beef-suet, and bees-wax melted together. Instead of a leather belt, ladies use a cord and tassels round the waist, to which the pouch, of a different shape to that adopted by gentlemen, is hooked; and this, again, has the grease-pot suspended to it.

The arm is protected from the blow of the string by the brace, a broad guard of strong leather buckled on by two straps. A shooting-glove, also of thin tubes of leather, is attached to the wrist by three flat pieces ending in a circular strap buckled round it. This glove prevents that soreness of the fingers which soon comes on after using the bow without it.

The target consists of a circular thick mat of straw covered with canvas, painted in a series of circles. It is usually from three feet six inches to four feet in diameter; the middle is about six or eight inches in diameter, gilt, and called "the gold;" the next is called "the red," after which comes the "inner white," then "the black," and finally, "the outer white." These targets are mounted upon triangular stands, at distances apart of from 50 to 100 yards; 60 being the usual shooting distance.

A scoring-card is provided with columns for each colour, which are marked with a pin, as here indicated. The usual score for a gold hit, 9; the red, 7; inner white, 6; black, 3, and outer white, 1.

★★★★★★

THE USE OF THE BOW.

To bend and string the bow properly, the following directions will be serviceable, and the young archer should pay particular attention to them, since a neglect of these cautions will often lead to a fracture of the bow by bending it the wrong way:

Take the bow by the *handle*, in the *right* hand.

Place the bottom end upon the ground, resting against the hollow of the inside of the right foot, keeping the flat side of the bow (called the *back*) towards your person; the left foot should be advanced a little, and the right placed so that the bow cannot slip sideways.

Place the heel of the left hand upon the upper limb of the bow, below the eye of the string. Now, while the fingers and thumb of the left hand slide this eye towards the notch in the horn, and the heel *pushes* the limb away from the body, the right hand *pulls* the handle towards the person, and thus resists the action of the left, by which the bow is bent, and at the same time the string is slipped into the "nock," as the notch is termed.

Take care to keep the three outer fingers free from the string, for if the bow should slip from the hand, and the string catch them, they will be severely pinched. If shooting in frosty weather, warm the bow before a fire, or by friction with a woollen cloth. If the bow has been lying by for a long time, it should be well rubbed with boiled linseed oil before using.

To unstring the bow, hold it as in stringing; then press down the upper limb exactly as before, and as if you wished to place the eye of the string in a higher notch; this will loosen the string and liberate the eye, when it must be lifted out of the nock by the forefinger, and suffered to slip down the limb.

Before using the bow, hold it in a perpendicular direction, with the string towards you, and see if the line of the string cuts the middle of the bow; if not, shift the eye and noose of the string to either side, so as to make the two lines coincide. This precaution prevents a very common cause of defective shooting, which is the result of an uneven string throwing the arrow on one side.

After using it, unstring it; and if a large party is shooting, after every end it should be liberated from its state of tension; but in this respect there is a great difference in different bows, some good ones soon getting cast from their true shape, and others, though inferior bows, bearing any ordinary amount of tension without damage.

The general management of the bow should be on the principle that damp injures it, and that any loose floating ends interfere with its shooting.

It should, therefore, be kept well varnished, and in a waterproof case, and it should be carefully dried after shooting in damp weather. If there are any ends hanging from the string cut them off pretty close, and see that the whipping in the middle of the string is close and well-fitting. The case should be hung up against a dry internal wall, not too near fire.

In selecting the bow, be careful that it is not too strong for your power, and that you can draw the arrow to its head without any trembling of the hand. If this cannot be done after a little practice, the bow should be changed for a weaker one, for no arrow will go true if it is discharged by a trembling hand.

In selecting arrows, be careful that they are not too long. For a bow of 5 feet 10 inches, the arrows should be about 2 feet 4 inches in length. For a lady's bow of 4 feet 10 inches, the arrow should measure about 2 feet.

In shooting, keep the longer limb of the bow upwards, as the bow is liable to be broken if used the other way, and the wrapping of the string does not coincide with the upper part of the handle. Bows may be broken either from the above circumstance, or by overdrawing them, or by snapping the string without an arrow in it, or by the string breaking; and if a bow stands all these trials, it is to be prized as a sound and good bit of stuff.

After an arrow has been shot into the target or the ground, be particularly careful to withdraw it, by laying hold close to its head, and by twisting it round as it is withdrawn in the direction of its axis. Without this precaution it may be easily bent or broken.

In shooting at the target, the first thing to be done is to nock the arrow—that is, to place it properly on the string. In order to effect this, take the bow in the left hand, with the string towards you, the upper limb being towards the right. Hold it horizontally while you take the arrow by the middle, pass it on the *under* side of the string and the *upper* side of the bow, till the head reaches two or three inches past the left hand; hold it there with the forefinger or thumb while you remove the right hand down to the nock. Turn the arrow till the cock-feather comes uppermost; then pass it down the bow, and fix it on the nocking point of the string. In doing this, all contact with the feathers should be avoided, unless they are rubbed out of place, when they may be smoothed down by passing them through the hand from the point towards the nock.

The Attitude for shooting should be graceful as well as serviceable. The body should be at right angles with the target; but the face must be turned over the left shoulder, so as to be opposed to it. The feet are to be flat on the ground, with the heels a little apart, the left foot turned towards the mark; the head and chest inclined a *little* forward, so as to present a full bust, but not bent at all below the waist.

In drawing the bow, proceed as follows:

1st Method.—Take hold of the bow with the left hand, having the elbow straight; then, having placed the arrow as directed in the last paragraph, and having the finger-stalls or shooting-glove on, put a finger on each side of the arrow on the string and the thumb on the opposite side, so as to steady it; then raise all at the full length of the arm till the right hand reaches nearly to the level of the shoulder, and the left is opposite the target, when, by drawing the one to the ear, and the other towards the target, the arrow is brought to a direct line with the bull's-eye, and at that moment it is released.

2nd Method.—Draw the arrow as before, but pause when the arrow is fully extended to the head, and take aim. This, however, requires a very strong arm, and also a strong bow, or there will be a quivering of the muscles, which is communicated to the arrow; beside the danger of breaking the bow. The loosing must be quick, and the string must leave the fingers smartly and steadily, the bow hand at that moment being held as firm as a vise, upon which the goodness of the flight mainly depends.

The following directions should be attended to strictly, if good shooting is to be attained:—

1.—Fix the attention steadily upon the object, and disregard all external objects, which are liable otherwise to distract the eye at the moment of shooting.

2.—In drawing the bow, in order to secure the arrow in its place, turn the bow a little obliquely, so that the handle and your knuckles will together form a groove for the arrow to run in. When it falls off, it is from the string being held too far up by the fingers, which causes it to twist in the drawing, and the arrow is thereby thrown off from resting against the bow. The proper length is midway between the ends and the first joint of the fingers. Three fingers may be used, but the arrow should be between the first and second.

3.—In taking aim, two points must be attended to, viz: the lateral *direction* and the *distance*, because there is no bow which will drive an arrow many yards perfectly *point-blank*, and, consequently, a slight elevation must in all cases be made, and for long distances, with weak bows, a very considerable one. It requires great experience to manage the elevation properly, and much must depend upon the exact strength of the bow, and the distance of the shot. With regard to the lateral direction, it is materially affected by the wind, and this must always be allowed for if there is any stirring; and if it is in the line of the targets, one end will require much less elevation than the other.

4.—Fix the eyes on the mark, and not on the arrow. Avoid all such expedients as putting a mark on the glove to aim by. Do not look from the mark to the arrow and back again. The proper plan is to keep both eyes open, and look steadily at the mark, while with the hands the bow is raised or lowered in accordance with what the *mind thinks* is the proper direction.

5.—If an arrow falls off the string, and the archer can reach it with his bow, it is not shot: but if he cannot, it must be counted as such.

TARGET-SHOOTING.

The Targets are fixed exactly opposite each other, at 60 yards or perhaps more apart. The stands, when properly placed, are each called "an end." The proper number of arrows, as fixed by the rules, are then shot from each end by all the party assembled, when all proceed to pick up or extract their arrows, the marker scoring for each before drawing them from the target, after which the party shoot back again to the other end, and so on until the whole number of ends have been shot.

BUTT-SHOOTING.

Butts are built of long sods of turf pressed together. The form of the base is an oblong square, being about 8 or 9 feet on the front side, and 5 feet wide at the ends. The height is generally about 7 feet, and the depth diminishes gradually from the bottom to the top. When more than two are wanted they are ranged in sets; each set consists of four, ranged at the distance of 30 yards apart, and forming a chain of lengths of 30, 60, 90, and 120 yards; but so disposed as not to stand in the way of the archers when shooting at any of the lengths.

Against the front of the butt is placed the mark, which is a circular piece of thin white pasteboard, fastened by a peg through the middle. The size of this, for 30 yards, is four inches in diameter; for 60 yards, 8 inches; and so on increasing in diameter in proportion to the distance. Shots in the butt missing the mark are not scored; and he who makes the greatest number of hits is the winner. If two are alike, the nearest to the central peg is the successful one.

ROVING.

This is so called because the archers rove from place to place, and have no fixed target, but shoot at trees or any other object which presents itself. The winner of the first shot chooses the next, and so on; the distance being from 100 to 200 yards; and all arrows falling within five bow-lengths scoring, if nearer to the mark than the adversary's arrow.

Flight-Shooting.

Flight-Shooting is merely a trial of distance, and he who can shoot the furthest is the winner of the trial.

Clout-Shooting.

The Clout is a small white target of pasteboard, about twelve inches in diameter, which is slipped into a cleft stick, and this is stuck into the ground obliquely, so as to bring the lower edge of the clout to the ground. The distance is generally from 8 to 10 score-yards, and the same rules apply as in roving.

Cross-bow Shooting.

Cross-bows are bows set in a frame which receives the arrow or bolt, and they are set and discharged by a trigger after taking aim. They are, however, now seldom used except for rook-shooting; and even there the pea-rifle has almost entirely superseded them.

Rules of Archery Meetings.

The rules by which archery meetings are governed are partly the same as in all other similar societies, and partly peculiar to this craft. The former consist of those which regulate the election of members, providing for refreshments, &c., which vary according to circumstances, and need not here be specified. The latter are generally as follows:—

1.—That a "lady paramount" be annually elected.

2.—That there be — meetings in each year, the gentleman at whose house the meeting takes place to be president; and that every member intending to shoot should be on the ground by — o'clock. The shooting to commence at — and to terminate at —.

3.—That all members intending to shoot shall appear in

the uniform of the club; and that a silver badge be worn by every member of the society, or a forfeit will be enforced for such omission.

4.—That the secretary do send out cards at least a month before each day of meeting, acquainting the members with the day and place of meeting.

5.—That there shall be four prizes at each meeting, two for each sex; the first for numbers, the second for hits, and that no person shall be allowed to have both on the same day. The sum of —— dollars to be placed at the disposal of the "lady paramount" for prizes at each meeting.

6.—That the winner of a prize, or prizes, shall lose a ring for each prize won. But that a ring be given back after any subsequent meeting at which such member shall shoot without winning.

7.—That in case of a tie for hits, numbers shall decide; and in case of a tie for numbers, hits shall decide.

8.—That the decision of the "lady paramount" shall be final.

9.—Two prizes to be given at each meeting for strangers, of the value of —.

10.—That there be a challenge prize of the value of —, and that a commemorative silver ornament be presented to winners of the challenge prize, to which a clasp be added on future occasions.

11.—That the distance for shooting be 60 and 100 yards, and that 4-feet targets be used.

12.—That each shooter be allowed to shoot — arrows, distinctly marked or coloured.

DRESS.

The usual dress for ladies peculiar to archery is in most cases a green jacket worn over white; sometimes, however, the colour is black.

The gentlemen's costume is not generally fixed in archery

clubs, but sometimes a green suit is the club uniform.

The expenses of archery are not usually grea, though a good many arrows will be lost or spoiled during a season's shooting, especially if the grass is not kept mown very close. Bows and all the other paraphernalia last a long while; and, with the exception of the arrows, the first cost may be considered to be the only one, over and above the subscription to the club, to which most archers like to belong, competition being the essence of the sport.

Hurdle Racing

1. The usual distance, 120 yards, over ten hurdles, regulation height, three feet six inches upright, not less than 12 or more than 20 feet apart, first hurdle must be placed 15 yards from the scratch-mark.

2. Hurdles must be cleared with a jump, touching the hands to the hurdle will be declared foul, and the offender disqualified.

3. Hurdle races may be arranged for any distance and any height of hurdle.

4. Each contestant must keep in his direct line of starting, or as near so as circumstances will permit. Any deviation from such line will subject the offender to disqualification.

Note.—There are three requisites to make a good hurdler: Speed, spring, and judgment; speed to cover the ground, spring to jump the hurdles, and judgment to measure the steps between the hurdles. It is one of the many healthful exercises in athletics, but requires much practice and experience; beginners should make their first effort at two feet six inches. Great care must be taken not to touch the top bar, as it virtually throws you out of the race and may cause injury.

Vaulting With Pole, or Pole-Leaping

1. The uprights should be nine feet apart, and the bar placed on pins projecting two inches.

2. The pole must fall so as not to touch the bar.

3. A competitor touching the bar without causing it to fall shall be considered to have cleared it.

4. The height of bar at starting shall be determined by a majority of the contestants.

5. Competitors will be allowed three trials at each height.

6. The bar shall be raised at the discretion of a majority of the contestants, and so continued until only one competitor vaults over it, who shall be declared the victor.

7. When a competitor knocks the bar down, the rotation rule must be enforced, as in the running high jump.

8. Three balks shall be called "no vault," and must be recorded as one of the three trials.

Note.—This graceful and manly exercise has of late years been greatly abused, not so much for want of rules, as it was and is to have these rules enforced. We have seen two men, at three different meetings, claim the right to the grounds and time of at least one of the judges for from two to three hours, whereas, had the rules been strictly enforced, one would have gained a victory or both been disqualified. Gentlemen Judges, please remember these contestants appear before an audience (who pay admission) to perform, not to practice, and when they insist upon keeping the bar at a height that delays the games, they should be disqualified under the rules.

Throwing the Hammer

1. The hammer-head shall be of solid iron, perfectly round, standard weights, 16 and 12 pounds, exclusive of handle. Length of handle three feet six inches over all. The handle should be made from split *white hickory wood*.

2. The competitor must stand at the scratch with one foot touching the scratch-mark. He is at liberty to throw with one or both hands.

3. Touching the ground, over the scratch-mark, with any portion of the body before the hammer strikes, shall be declared "no throw," and must be recorded as one of the three trials.

4. Permitting the hammer to carry a competitor from his balance or letting the hammer go out of time must stand as one of the three trials.

5. When the head and handle strike the ground at the same time the head or iron is the measuring mark, at the first break of the ground made by it. Should the handle strike first, one length of the handle, in a direct line with the throw, must be[Pg 60] added. The measurement must be from the scratch-mark, midway between the thrower's feet, to the first break, in accordance with above rules.

Note.—In soft or clay bottom there is no difficulty in getting accurate measurement, but in quick or shifting sand close attention is required.

Putting the Shot

1. The shot must be of solid iron and perfectly round, standard weight 16 pounds. The shot must be put from the shoulder with one hand, not thrown from the side or under swing.

2. Competitors will take their position between two parallel lines, said lines being seven feet apart. Passing the toe-mark, or touching the ground outside of the mark, with any part of the body before the shot strikes the ground, will be judged and recorded a foul, "no put," and must stand as one of the three trials.

3. Each competitor is entitled to three trials. The measurement shall be from the scratch-line or mark opposite the toe-print to the first or nearest break of the ground made by the shot.

Note.—The object being to see how many feet and inches the competitors can put, in accordance with the above rules, not how straight they can put.

A New System of Broad and
Small Sword Exercise

Contents

General Introduction

The author feels confident that his labours will receive the approval of every true American citizen who regards the profession of arms as necessary to a sure national defence; as well as all others who look upon the diffusion of military art, among the people at large, as one of the best securities for the permanency of our Republican Institutions.

The "Soldier," and the "Citizen Soldier," will deem no long-winded and verbose introduction necessary, as an inducement to call their attention to the work. The author frankly asks them to examine the following pages for their own satisfaction; he cheerfully challenges comparison between his system of Instruction and any other system at present in existence.

The merit of the work consists in acknowledged improvements, originated and perfected by the author, from observation, long and thorough practice, and a familiar acquaintance with the use of every species of modern weapon, acquired in the schools of European service.

The want of an uniform system of sword exercise in this country is apparent to every military man; therefore, nothing need be added on this head.

The advice and recommendations of numerous friends, military men, officers high in rank, and various gentlemen of station, intelligence, and military skill, coupled with a desire to establish a complete sword manual, induced the compilation of the present work—which the author now offers to the public.

DEDICATED,
WITH MUCH RESPECT, TO THE
MILITARY OF THE UNITED STATES,
BY THEIR FELLOW CITIZEN,
THOMAS STEPHENS.

CHAPTER 1

Instruction of the Cavalry Soldier on Foot

INTRODUCTORY REMARKS.

The instructors, to whom this duty is intrusted, ought to possess accurate knowledge of every part which is to be taught, and convey their instructions in such a clear, firm, and concise manner, as will command a perfect attention to their directions. They should make allowance for the weak capacity of the recruit; be patient, not rigorous, where endeavour and good will are apparent; for quickness is the result of much practice, and ought not at first to be expected.

Recruits should be carried on progressively; they should understand one thing before they proceed to another. In the first circumstances of position, the limbs should be justly placed by the instructor; when more advanced, they should not be touched; but from the example shown, and the directions given, they must be taught to correct themselves. Recruits should not be kept too long at any particular part of their exercise, so as to fatigue or to make them uneasy.

In the manner hereafter prescribed, recruits ought to be trained singly, or in squads, until they are perfect in all points of exercise.

SECTION 1
EXTENSION MOTIONS.

These motions tend to expand the chest, raise the head, throw back the shoulders, and strengthen the muscles of the back.

POSITIONS OF THE SOLDIER.

The equal squareness of the shoulders and body to the front, is the first and great principle of the position of a soldier. The heels must be in a line, and closed; the knees straight, without stiffness; the toes a little turned out, so that the feet may form an angle of about sixty degrees; the arms hanging near the body, without stiffness; the elbows close to the sides; palms of the hands turned a little to the front; the little fingers behind the seams of the pantaloons; the stomach rather drawn in, and the breast advanced, but without constraint; the body upright, but inclining forward, so that the weight of it may principally bear on the fore part of the feet; the head to be erect, and neither turned to the right nor left.

OPEN INTERVAL

Is taken by each recruit stretching out his right arm so as to touch the left shoulder of his right-hand man, and keeping that distance from him.

STANDING AT EASE.

On the word "Stand at ease," the right foot is drawn back about six inches—hollow of the foot opposite the heel of the left. Cross the hands naturally in front; palm of the right grasping the back of the left; the elbows a little bent.

ATTENTION.

On the word "Attention," briskly resume the first position. When the recruit falls in for instruction, he is first to be taught to place himself, on the word "Fall in," in the position above described, to remain perfectly silent, and to give his whole attention to his instructor. Occasionally during the time of drill the recruit should be allowed to rest by "Standing at ease."

SECTION 2
PACING AND MARCHING.—EYES TO THE FLANK.

Eyes Right.—On the word "Eyes Right," glance the eyes to the right, with the slightest turn possible of the head. At the word "Eyes Left," cast the eyes in like manner to the left. On the word "Eyes Front," the look and head are to be directly to the front, the habitual position of the soldier.

Particular attention must be paid, in the several turnings of the eyes, to prevent the soldier from moving his body, which should be preserved perfectly square to the front. In all marches to the front, the pupil or recruit is to be taught to keep his eyes steadily fixed, as if looking at some object of his own height, at one hundred yards distance in front; and the eyes are never to be cast down, or thrown to a flank, except when ordered. On all other occasions, the touch of the pupil or recruit must be his guide.

The Facings.

In going through the facings, the left heel never quits the ground; the body must rather incline forward, and the knees be kept straight.

Right Face.—1st. Place the hollow of the right foot smartly against the left heel, keeping the shoulders square to the front. 2nd. Raise the toes, and turn to the right on both heels.

Left Face.—1st. Place the right heel against the hollow of the left foot, keeping the shoulders square to the front. 2nd. Raise the toes, and turn to the left on both heels.

Right-about Face.—1st. Place the ball of the right toe against the left heel, keeping the shoulders square to the front, 2nd. Raise the toes, and turn to the right-about on both heels. 3rd. Bring the right foot smartly back in a line with the left.

Left-about Face.—Place the right heel against the ball of the left toe, keeping the shoulders square to the front. 2nd. Raise the toes, and turn to the left-about on both heels.

Right or Left, Half Face.—Each man will make an exact half face, as directed, by drawing back or advancing the right foot one inch, by which the whole will stand individually in echellons.

Instruction of Front.

Front.—The whole will face, as accurately as possible, to

their former front.

Might or Left-about, Three quarters Face.—The recruit brings the ball of the right foot to the left heel, or the right heel to the ball of the left foot, and makes a three quarters face in the given direction. Upon the word "Front," if he has faced to the right, he fronts to the left; and if he has faced to the left, he fronts to the right.

The feet, in the first of the above motions, are to be slipped back or brought forward without a jerk, the movement being from the hip, so that the body is kept perfectly steady until faced.

The greatest precision must be observed in these facings, for if they are not exactly executed, a body of men, after being properly dressed, will lose their dressing on every small movement of facing.

Position in Marching.

In marching, the soldier must maintain, as much as possible, the position of the body, as directed in section 1. He must be well balanced on his limbs. His arms and hands, without stiffness, must be kept steady by his side, and not suffered to vibrate. He must not be allowed to stoop forward, or to lean back. His body must be kept square to the front, and thrown rather more forward in marching than when halted, that it may accompany the movement of the leg and thigh; which movement must spring from the haunch. The ham must be stretched, but without stiffening the knee; the toe a little pointed, and kept near the ground, so that the shoe soles may not be visible to a person in front; the head to be kept well up, straight to the front, and the eyes not suffered to be cast down; the foot, without being drawn back, must be placed flat on the ground.

Balance Step, Without Gaining Ground.

Front.—The left foot is brought gently forward, with the toe at the proper angle to the left, the foot about three inches from the ground, the left heel in line with the toe of the right foot.

Rear.—When steady, the left foot is brought gently back,

(without a jerk,) the left knee a little bent, the left toe brought close to the right heel. The left foot, in this position, will not be so flat as to the front, as the toe will be a little depressed.

When steady, the words "Front" and "Rear" will be given alternately, and repeated three or four times. To prevent the pupils or recruits being fatigued, the word "Halt" will be given—when the left foot, either advanced or to the rear, will be brought to the right. The instructor will afterward make the pupil or recruit balance upon the left leg, advancing or retiring the right in the same manner.

BALANCE STEP, GAINING GROUND BY THE WORD "FORWARD."

On the word "Front," the left foot is brought smartly to the front as before; the knee straight, the toe turned out a little to the left, and remaining about three inches from the ground. In this pasture he remains for a few seconds only in the first instance, till practice has steadied him in the position.

Forward.—On this word the left foot is brought to the ground, at thirty inches from heel to heel,, while the right foot is raised at the same moment, and continues extended to the rear. The body remains upright, but inclining forward; the head erect, and neither turned to the right nor left.

On the word "Two," the right foot is brought forward in a line with the left, the toe a little turned out, and the sole quite flat, but raised two inches from the ground.

On the word "Front," the right foot is brought forward, and so on.

BALANCE STEP IN DOUBLE TIME.

The balance step in double time is performed in the manner last described, but without the word of command for each step, the instructor merely giving the words "Double time—March." The pupil or recruit judges his own time, going through distinctly the balance of each leg; and when the Instructor observes that he is steady, the time is gradually decreased to the slow step.

In the balance step the toe is not to be pointed, or any flourish made with the foot, which is to be placed flat on the ground, without shaking the body.

With a view to determine the exact length of pace required from the pupil or recruit, in the above movements, the pace stick must be used to measure and regulate his step according to the time required.

Slow Step.

The length of each pace, from heel to heel, is thirty inches, and the pupil or recruit must be taught to take seventy-five of these steps in a minute, without tottering, and with perfect steadiness. He must be thoroughly instructed in this step, as an essential foundation for arriving at accuracy in the quicker paces. This is the slowest step at which troops are to move, and will be applied to movements of parade.

Halting.

On the word "Halt," let the rear foot be brought upon a line with the advanced one,, so as to finish the step which was taken when the command was given.

N. B.—The words "Halt—front," "Halt—dress," are each to be considered as one word of command, and no pause made between the parts of their execution.

Section 3
Instruction for a Squad in Single Rank.

Three or four pupils, or recruits, will now be formed in one rank, at very open files, and instructed as follows:

Stepping Out.

The squad marches, as already directed, in slow time; on the word "Step out," the pupil or recruit must be taught to lengthen his step to thirty-three inches, by leaning forward a little, but without altering the cadence.

This step is necessary when a temporary increase of pace is required, and is applied both to slow and quick time; and, at the word "Slow," or "Quick step," the pace of thirty inches must be resumed.

Stepping Short.

On the word "Step short," the foot advancing will finish its pace, and afterward each pupil or recruit will step as far as the ball of his toe, and no farther, until the word "Forward" be given, when the usual step of thirty inches is to be taken.

This step is useful when a momentary decrease of pace is required.

Marking Time.

On the word "Mark time," the foot then advancing completes its pace; after which the cadence is continued, without gaining any ground, but alternately throwing out the foot and bringing it back square with the other. At the word "Forward," the usual pace of thirty inches will be taken.

This step is necessary when a column, division, (fee, on the march, has to wait for the coming up of others.

Stepping Back.

The "Step back" is performed in the slow time and length of pace from the halt. On the command "Step back—march," the pupil or recruit must be taught to move straight to the rear, preserving his shoulders square to the front, and his body erect. On the word "Halt," the foot in front must be brought back square with the other. A few paces only of the "Step back" can be necessary at a time.

Changing the Feet.

Change Feet.—The advanced foot completes its pace, the ball of the other is brought up quickly to the heel of the advanced one, which instantly makes another step forward, so that the cadence may not be lost.

This may be required of a man who is stepping with a different foot from the rest of his division: in doing" which he will in fact take two successive steps with the same foot.

The Quick Step.

The cadence of the "Slow pace" having become perfectly habitual to the pupil or recruit, he is now to be taught to march in "Quick time," which is one hundred and eight steps in a minute, each of thirty inches, making two hundred and seventy feet in a minute.

Quick March.—The command "Quick march" is to be given with a pause between the words; the word "quick" being considered as a caution, and the whole remaining perfectly still and steady. On the word "march," they step off with the left foot, keeping the body in the same posture, and the shoulders square to the front; the foot to be lifted off the ground, that it may clear any stones or other impediments in the way, and to be thrown forward and placed firm; the whole of the sole to touch the ground, and not the heel alone; the knees are to be bent a little, so as not to occasion fatigue or restraint; the arms to hang with ease down the outside of the thigh; the head is to be kept to the front, the body well up, and the utmost steadiness to be observed.

After the pupil or recruit is perfectly grounded in marching to the front in quick time, all the alterations of step, as above, for slow time, must be practiced in the quick time.

This is the pace which will be applied generally to all movements by large as well as small bodies of troops; and, therefore, the pupil or recruit must be thoroughly trained in this important part of his instruction.

THE SIDE, OR CLOSING STEP.

The Side, or closing step, is performed from the halt in quick time, by the following command: *Right close,—Quick march; Left close,—Quick march.*

In closing to the right, on the "Quick march," eyes are turned to the right, and each man carries his right foot about ten inches directly to his right, (or if the files are closed, to the next man's left foot,) and instantly brings up his left foot till the heel touches his right heel, and proceeds to take the next step in the same manner; the whole with perfect precision of time, shoulders kept square, knees not bent, and in the true line on which the body is formed. At the word "Halt," the whole halt, turn their eyes to the front, and are perfectly steady.

Marching Straight-Forward.

To march "Straight-forward" is of the utmost consequence, and the Instructor will take the greatest care to make his squad perfect in this essential object; for this purpose he will often place himself behind the flank file by which the squad is to move in marching; he will then command "march," and, remaining in his place, will direct the advance of the squad, by keeping the flank file always in a line with the points upon which he has directed it to march. It is also from the rear that the leaning back of the soldier, and the bringing forward or falling back of a shoulder, are soonest perceived; faults which, if not instantly rectified, will create confusion in a line; where one man, by bringing forward a shoulder, may quite change the direction of the march.

In short, it is impossible to labour too much at making the soldier more straight-forward, keeping always the same front as when he commenced his march. This is effected by moving solely from the haunches, keeping always the body steady, the shoulders square, and the head to the front; and it will be attained without difficulty by a strict attention to the rules given for marching, and a careful observance of an equal length of step, and an equal cadence, or time of march.

Right or left turn must be often ordered on the march, in order to practice divisions when moving in file, to front and move forward without halting; or when moving in front, to make them move on in file.

Right or left-about turn, changes the front on the march without halting. On the word "turn," each individual soldier, without changing step or cadence, comes to the right or left-about on his own ground, and in his own person, performing the movement in the time prescribed for three distinct paces, then marking time till he receives the word "forward," when he resumes the full pace to the front.

Inclining.

When the squad is marching to the front, and it is desired to take an oblique direction, the word "Right, or left half- turn" is given, and the men move on the oblique lines upon which they are individually placed in echelon, as described in the half facings. When it is intended to move to the original front without halting, the word "Front turn" is given, when each man will turn his body to the front, and move forward without checking the pace.

During the incline the dressing is to that hand to which the incline is made; therefore, when a division is moving by the right half-turn, the right hand man must pay particular attention to the length of pace, and to move straight on the line he took up when he made his half-turn, as the accuracy of his movement assists very much in keeping the division in its proper position. The other files must be careful that their right arms do not get beyond the centre of the men's backs who are on their right; and if they keep this position, their right feet will just clear the left of the preceding file.

The instruction for the incline should commence on a single rank without arms.

THE DOUBLE MARCH.

The directions for the march already given, apply in a great degree to this step, which is 150 steps in the minute, each of 36 inches, making 450 feet in a minute.

On the word "*Double march*" the whole step off together with the left feet, keeping the heads erect, and the shoulders square to the front; the knees are a little bent, the ball of the foot only need be brought to the ground. The body is more advanced than in the other marches; the arms hang with ease down the outside of the thigh, as in the quick march.

The greatest care must always be taken that the pupil or recruit shall step off at and preserve the full pace of 36 inches, which can be done with ease, if the soldier is properly placed in position, as directed in section 1, and that the weight of the body inclines well forward on the fore part of the feet.

DIFFERENCE OF STEP.

The word "March," given singly, at all times denotes that

"Slow time" is to be taken; when the "Quick," or "Double march" is meant, the word "Quick" or "Double," will precede the word "March." Recruits, or pupils, should be much practiced in changing the time on the march, except from "Double" to "Slow," which should never be done without a previous halt.

Three or four pupils or recruits in one rank, with intervals of twelve inches between them, should be practiced in the different steps, that they may acquire a firmness and independence of movement.

MEASUREMENT OF STEP.

Plummets, which vibrate the required times of march in a minute, are of great utility, and can alone prevent or correct uncertainty of movement; they must be in the possession, and constantly referred to by each instructor of a squad. The several lengths of plummets, swinging the times of the different marches in a minute, are as follows:

	In.	Hun.
Slow time, 75 steps in the minute,	24	96
Quick time, 108 " "	12	3
Double march, 150 " "	6	26

A musket-ball suspended by a string which is not subject to stretch, and on which are marked the different lengths, will answer the above purpose, and should be frequently compared with an accurate standard in the adjutant's or sergeant-major's possession. The length of the plummet is to be measured from the point to the centre of the ball.

CLOSE ORDER.

Six or eight pupils or recruits will now be formed in rank, at close files, each lightly touching to the dressing hand, with a steady, well drilled soldier on their flank to lead, and are to be instructed as follows:

DRESSING WHEN HALTED.

Dressing is to be taught equally by the left as by the right. On the word "Dress," each individual will cast his eyes to the point to which he is ordered to "dress," with the smallest turn possible of the head, but preserving the shoulders and body square to their front. The whole person of the man must move as may be necessary, and bending backward or forward is not to be permitted. He must take short, quick steps, thereby gradually and exactly to gain his position, and on no account be suffered to attempt it by any sudden or violent alteration, which must infallibly derange whatever is beyond him. The faces of the men, and not their breasts or feet, are the line of dressing.

Each man is to be able just to distinguish the surface of the face of the second man beyond him. The faults generally committed by the soldier in dressing are, passing the line; the head too forward and body kept back; the shoulders not square; the head turned too much. To avoid these the following instructions will be observed in the drill of pupils or recruits:

The two right-hand men will be moved up a pace and a half; the instructor will then give the word "Right dress," when the third pupil or recruit will take a pace to the front with the left foot, and shuffle up into line with the two points on his right, taking up his touch and dressing at the same time; the instructor standing clear to the right of the two points, when he sees that the pupil or recruit is properly dressed, and the touch perfect, give the word "Eyes front," that heads may be replaced and remain square to the front.

When every recruit, individually, has practiced, and is perfect in his dressing up, both by right and left forward, he must be taught to dress up and back together, taking care that the touch is always preserved, and afterward the whole squad together.

No rank or body ought ever to be dressed, without the person on its flank appointed to dress it, determining, or at least supposing a line on which the rank or body is to be formed, and for that purpose taking as the object a point beyond the distant or outward flank; his dressing must then be made gradually and progressively from the inward flank toward the outer one.

File Marching.

Right/Left Face.—The recruits must first face, and then be instructed to cover each other exactly in file, so that the head of the man immediately before may conceal the heads of all the others in his front. The strictest observance of all the rules for marching is particularly necessary in marching by file, which is first to be taught at the slow time, and afterwards in quick time.

On the word "March," the whole are immediately to step off together, gaining at the very first step thirty inches, and so continue each step without increasing the distance between each recruit, every man locking or placing his advanced foot on the ground, before the spot from whence his preceding man had taken up his—no looking down, nor leaning backward, is to be suffered—the leader is to be directed to march straight forward to some distant object given him for that purpose, or recruits made to cover one another, during the march, with the most scrupulous exactness; great attention must be paid to prevent them from marching with their knees bent, which they will be very apt to do at first from an apprehension of treading upon the heels of those before them,

WHEELING OF A SINGLE RANK FROM THE HALT.

At the word "Right wheel," the man on the right of the rank faces to the right, on the word "March" they step off together, the whole turning their eyes to the left, (the wheeling flank,) except the man on the left of the rank, who looks inward. The outward wheeling man steps the usual pace of thirty inches, and the whole observe the same time, but each man shortening his step in proportion as he is nearer to the standing flank on which the wheel is made; during the wheel, the whole remain closed to the standing flank, that is, they touch without pressing; they must not stoop forward, but remain up- right. Opening out from the standing flank is to be avoided; closing in upon it, during the wheel, is to be resisted.

On the word "Halt—Dress," each man halts immediately, and dresses to the standing flank. The dressing being completed, the squad receives the command "Eyes front." When the pupils or recruits are able to perform the wheel with accuracy in the slow time, they must be practiced in quick time.

Nothing will tend sooner to enable the recruit to acquire the proper length of step, according to his distance from the pivot, than continuing the wheel without halting for several circles, and also giving the word "Halt—Dress," at instants not expected, and when only a part of the circle is completed.

Wheeling Backward a Single Rank.

At the words on the "Right, backward wheel," the man on the right of the rank faces to his left. At the word "quick march," the whole step backward in quick time, and observe the same attention as in wheeling forward. The recruits should be first practiced to wheel backward at the slow step; and at all times it will be necessary to prevent them from hurrying the pace—an error soldiers are very liable to fall into, particularly in wheeling backward. This wheeling is necessary o preserve the covering of the pivot flanks when large bodies wheel from line into column for the purpose of prolonging the alignment.

Changing the Direction Upon the March.

When the rank is marching to the front, and is to change its direction to either flank, it receives the word "Right" (or "Left)"; upon which the outward file of the named flank continues to step out at the full pace, and the wheeling is performed by bringing the shoulder gradually round, and circling on the inward flank file, which marks time until the word "Forward," which is given by the commander as soon as he sees that the rank has gained the direction in which he intends it again to move forward.

Section 4

Instruction for a Squad in Double Ranks

Formation in Two Ranks.

The recruits being thoroughly grounded in the foregoing instructions, will now be practiced in two ranks; the rear rank being formed at one pace, *i. e.* 30 inches from the front rank, each man covering correctly, and looking at the middle of the neck of his front rank man, to which points his attention must be particularly directed in all marches and wheelings.

In file marching, in two ranks, the men of the rear rank must look to and regulate themselves by their front rank men. The squad, when marching in file, must be accustomed to wheel its head to either flank, each file following successively without alteration of distances. On this occasion each file makes a wheel on a pivot, movable in a very small degree, but without altering its time of march, or the eyes of the rear rank being turned from their front rank.

The wheel backward need not be practiced on uneven ground, or when the divisions are stronger than eighteen files. In such cases the divisions may face about, wheel, and then "*Halt—Front.*"

Opening and Closing the Ranks.

The recruits being formed in two ranks, at close order, on the word "Rear rank, take order," the flank men on the right and left of the rear rank step back two paces, face to their right, and stand covered to mark the ground on which the rear rank is to halt, and dress at open order , every other man remains ready to move. On the word "March," the flank men front, and the rear rank falls back two paces, dressing by the right the instant it is in its place.

On the word "Rear rank, take close order," the whole remain perfectly steady; at the word "March," the rank closes within one pace.

To Form Four Deep.

The division will be led off from the right by alternate files, right and left. When it is intended to form four deep, preserving the same front, the word "Form four deep" is given, on which the rear rank step back one pace; and on the word "March," the left files double behind the right files, by taking one pace to the rear with the left feet, and one pace to the right with the right feet.

Right, form Four Deep.—On this caution, the rear rank step back as before. On the word "March," the whole face to the right, and the left files, at the same instant, form on the right of the right files.

Left, form Four Deep.—On this caution, the rear rank step back as before. On the word "March," the whole face to the left, and the left files—at the same instant form on the left of the right files.

In all these formations the files preserve their proper order and place; and two deep is re-formed from each of them by the word "Front;" upon which the lines move up into line at their respective intervals. The rear rank immediately closes to the front.

The word "Halt" will precede the word "Front," if the division has been in movement.

In moving to a flank file, marching may be adopted, if necessary, by the files leading out in their proper order upon the word "Form two deep;" and at the word "Re-form four deep," resuming their former places.

Section 5
Practice of Cavalry Movements on Foot.

For this purpose the regiment is to be formed, and told off in the same manner as when mounted, and the same system will be pursued throughout. The officers are to be posted two paces in front of the squadron, and the rear rank at the like distance from the front rank. In increasing the front, the "Double time" will be used to represent the "Trot;" also in the wheels, when the pace of manoeuvre is "Quick time."

In the formations, one pace is to be allowed for a horse's length.

CHAPTER 2

The Broad Sword Exercise

SECTION 1
THE BROAD SWORD EXERCISE—DISMOUNTED

The broad sword exercise for Cavalry, to be well performed, should be often practiced when dismounted, by companies or squadrons, formed in line; the tallest men being placed on the right. When the line has been formed for drill, the instructor gives word—"Eyes right and dress;" "eyes front." The word "Stand at ease" having been given, the pupil is to draw the right foot back six inches, the greater portion of the body resting on the right leg; the hands to be brought together in front of the body, the right hand to grasp the left. This is the position "Stand at ease."

POSITION OF ATTENTION.

The Instructor gives the word, "Attention," and the pupil springs to that position, body erect, arms hanging easily by the sides, palms of the hands turned to the front, heels together, and toes inclined outward.

TO TAKE DISTANCE FOR SWORD EXERCISE

The right-hand man keeps his post; the remainder left passage, dressing to the right, standing at open interval of about five or six feet apart, will then halt, eyes front. The word is then given, "Prepare for cavalry broad sword exercise." Each pupil or recruit steps from eighteen to twenty inches to the right, standing at open position, imitating that of being mounted.

The sword exercise of cavalry has three divisions—arranged in reference to the different combinations of the cuts and thrusts, whether against infantry, cavalry, or both. The motions are all performed by presenting a proper front in the direction whence the attack would be received; and it is always from some quarter of the right or left side of the horse; as it would be impossible to meet an opponent face to face while sitting naturally in the saddle; but can only approach by passing side by side. In this view the motions will be made in directions either on the right or left, where the adversary is supposed to be.

Draw Swords.—Bring the hand smartly across the body to the sword-knot, place it on the wrist, and give the hand a couple of turns inward, in order to make it fast, and at the same time seize the hilt and raise the sword-blade six inches out of the scabbard; by a second motion extend the arm to the right, the point in an elevated position, edge to the right.

One.—Bring the sword hand in front of the cheek; sword erect, edge to the left.

Two.—Bring the sword to the carry, by dropping the arm to the hip; elbow and wrist horizontal, sword erect, with the edge to the front.

SLOPE SWORD.

Loosen the grasp of the handle, let the blade rest against the shoulder, with the edge of the blade-front sloping.

FIRST DIVISION OF PRACTICE.

Carry Sword.—Grasp the handle, and at the same time raise the sword from the shoulder perpendicularly.

GUARDS ON THE LEFT.

The same as on the right, only defending the left side. First defending the left cheek: second, defending the right cheek, or neck; third defending the left leg, (rear;) fourth, defending the left leg, (front;) fifth, defending the bridle arm, or horse's hind quarters; sixth, defending the bridle rein, or front part of the

No. 1.—GUARD.

Raise the arm full length, sloping the sword over the head, the point bearing over the left shoulder; point lower than the handle, the edge upward.

No. 2.—ASSAULT.

Cut One.—Raise the sword arm; the back of the sword in the hollow of the right shoulder; cut from front to rear, on the near side of the horse, at infantry.

Cut Two.—Change the direction of the body, place the back of the sword in the hollow of the left shoulder; cut from front to rear, on the off side of the horse, at infantry.

Cut Three.—Carry the sword arm to the right rear, the blade perpendicular; cut from rear to front, on the off side of the horse, at infantry.

Cut Four.—Carry the sword hand in the hollow of the left shoulder, opposite the breast; the blade perpendicular, the edge to the rear. Cut from rear to front, on the near side of the horse, at infantry.

Cut Five.—Carry the sword arm to the right, bearing the back of the sword against the collar of the coat. Cut from right to left at the bridle arm, or left side, at cavalry.

Cut Seven.—Raise the sword arm full length, throw the wrist to the rear, the back of the blade resting on the right shoulder. Cut to the front at cavalry.

Cut Six.—Change the direction of the body, cast the eyes to the right, place the flat of the sword on the left shoulder, the elbow and wrist in a line of direction. Cut to the right at defendant's sword arm, of cavalry.

POINTS.

First Point.—Raise the sword arm with the hand opposite the right eye ; the sword and arm in a line of direction, the edge upward, point to the left front.

Second Point.—Place the elbow inside the right hip-bone, the edge of the sword upward, the point to the right front *point* ; raise the wrist and lower the point.

Third Point.—Place the heel of the hand on the right hip-bone, the edge to the right front, the point elevated *point*; raise the wrist and lower the point.

First. To defend the Left Cheek on the left side of the neck.—*Position*; sword hand carried to the left, the point is to be opposite and above the right eye, the edge to the left front.

GUARDS.—SEVEN ON THE RIGHT.

SECOND. *To defend the Right Cheek on the right side of the neck.* Change the position to defend the right cheek or neck; place the sword arm to the right, the blade in a horizontal direction to the left, the point elevated.

THIRD. *To defend the Front Part of the Right Leg.*—Place the sword arm in front of the thigh, the edge to the front, the point to the rear.

FOURTH. *To defend the Haunch of the Bow-ing Part of the Leg.*—Bring the sword arm in rear of the right leg, the point to the front, edge to the right.

FIFTH. *To defend the Bridle Arm, or Left Side.*—Raise the sword arm directly in front of the brow, the hand over the left shoulder, the edge to the left, the point downward.

SIXTH. *To defend the Sword Arm or Right Side.*—Raise the sword arm to the right, as high as the head; the edge to the front, the point downward.

SEVENTH. *To defend the Head.*—Raise the sword arm full length over the head, the sword directing to the left, the edge upward, the point sloping over the left shoulder.

PARRIES ON THE RIGHT.

First Parry.—From front to rear, with the back of the sword.

Second Parry.—From rear to front with the back of the sword.

body; seventh, defending the head.

PARRIES ON THE LEFT.

First, from rear to front with the back of the sword; second, from front to rear. Carry sword; slope sword.

SECTION 3
SECOND DIVISION OF PRACTICE

Is performed by cuts in succession, and giving points on the same side. The four first cuts and points to be given at infantry; the remaining three points and cuts at cavalry.

ATTENTION.

Carry sword; Guard; Assault; Cut one; Point; Cut two; Point; Cut three; Point; Cut four; Point; Cut five; Point; Cut six; Point; Cut seven; Point.

SECTION 4
THIRD DIVISION OF PRACTICE

Is performed by cuts in succession, and giving points on the reverse side.

ATTENTION.

Carry sword; Guard; Assault; Cut one; Point; Cut two; Point; Cut three; Point; Cut four; Point; Cut five; Point; Cut six; Point; Cut seven; Point. Slope sword; stand at ease.

Attack.—Cut one, at the left cheek, or neck.

Defence.—Form the first guard, defending the left cheek, or neck.

Attack.—Cut two, at the right cheek, or neck.

Defence.—Form the second guard.

Attack.—Cut three, at the front part of the body.

Defence.—Form the third guard.

Attack.—Cut four, at the haunch, or bowing part of the leg.

Defence.—Form the fourth guard.

Attack.—Cut five, at the bridle arm, or left side of the

ATTACK AND DEFENCE, MOUNTED.

Cutting at Cavalry altogether; right attack—right engage.

POINTS.

body.

Defence.—Form the fifth guard.

Attack.—Cut six, at the sword arm, or right side of the body.

Defence.—Form the sixth guard.

Attack.—Cut seven, at the head, downward.

Defence.—Come to the seventh guard.

Attack.—First point, to the front, the back of the hand opposite the right cheek, the edge upward, pointing to the front.

Defence.—Parry from rear to front, the point upward, the edge to the front.

Attack.—Second point; place the elbow inside the hip-bone, the edge upward, the point elevated "point;" raise the wrist and lower the point.

Defence.—Raise the sword hand high as the brow, the back of the sword to the front; parry from front to rear.

Attack.—Third point; place the heel of the sword hand on the right hip-bone, the point elevated, the edge upward, "point;" raise the wrist and lower the point.

Defence.—Raise the sword hand high as the brow, the back of the sword to the front; parry from front to rear.

THE LEFT ATTACK AND LEFT ENGAGE

Are the same as the right, only attacking the left side. The guards and parries are the same, only on the left side.

SECTION 5
GENERAL OBSERVATIONS AND DIRECTIONS FOR SWORD EXERCISE.

The exercise of the broad sword consists of seven cuts, or directions of the edge; the same number of guards, or defensive positions; three points, or thrusts, given with the edge up, and with two circular motions of the blade, termed parries; therefore, whatever may be the attack or defence, it can only be formed by having recourse to some of the above movements, or a combination of them.

In "engaging" by which is meant the action of joining the sword of an opponent, either previous to his or your own attack, there should be only a slight pressure on his blade, so that the hand, or wrist, may be the more susceptible of any motion he may make; and though the position is termed "guard," affords protection at the moment, it is merely considered as preparatory to an offensive or defensive movement, varying the latter according to the points liable to be attacked.

In all attacks, whether cuts or thrusts, the motion ought to increase in speed, the impetus being at the last; the same rule should be observed in stepping out to the "second" and "third positions," but in recovering, the reverse is to be followed, as the first part is to be the quickest; and nothing can be of more importance than that the eye should follow those of an opponent, and slightly glance at the part at which you intend to cut or thrust—taking care never to look at your own sword, which will invariably follow the eye wherever you direct it.

It is merely drill practice, making the assault by numbers; and although each cut has its guard, according to the number, which answers for both, yet it does not follow that the file on the defensive is always to have recourse to it, as he may frequently be enabled to secure himself more effectively, and quicker, by forming another guard. If, for example, he makes the cut six at the body, and his opponent, after defending by the sixth guard, returns the cut one at the breast, then the fifth guard becomes the quickest movement of defence; but if the opponent has defined by the second guard, previous to his return of the cut one, then the first guard is the soonest formed; consequently, the first and fifth guards each defend the cuts one or five.

The second and sixth guards each defend the cuts two or six, according as they may be high or low; and if the third or fourth guards are required for the defence of the leg, the arm must be extended, so that the force of the blade may receive the foible of the opponent's weapon, bearing well in mind, however, that in all cuts at the leg, when at the proper distance, the shifting of your own leg and delivering a cut at the same moment, becomes the most effective and advantageous defence; and which is still more so to a tall man when engaged with another of lesser stature, or length of arm.

The power of defence does not, in fact, consist so much in your own strength of position, as in effecting a decided quick movement in that direction in which your opponent has the least power of resistance, especially in defending against the point, when the first, third and fifth guards are the most effective against the first and third point; and the second, fourth and sixth guards against the second point: provided the wrist is previously so placed that the requisite guards may be quickly executed. The two last parries must also be regulated by the position of the opponent's wrist, so that the bearing of your sword may tend to open his hand, and, if well judged and timely given, will disarm him, or so cripple his wrist, as to preclude even the capability of forming a defensive guard, or continuing the attack.

If opposed to the small sword, have recourse to the cuts three and four, directing them at the arm, by which means there is every probability of the cuts taking effect, as in thrusting, the arm must always come in range of the edge, before the point can be sufficiently advanced to reach the body. If the above cuts are quickly given and continued, they will be found advantageous in advancing against the small sword, as they form an attack and defence at the same instant; but should the opponent be the most skilful and quickest, then it is best to retire while forming them, cautiously preserving the proper distance, so that each cut may just reach the fore-part of his arm.

Thus far the observations are more particularly applicable to the first part of the instructions, or when practicing on foot, though they may generally answer for exercise also when mounted; and here the greatest attention should be paid to maintain the proper position and balance of the body, from which, by too great an exertion in delivering a cut or thrust, the horseman may suddenly be thrown, and thereby lose the advantage of his skill in the use of the sword, by the natural efforts which he must make to regain his seat; nor should he fail to have every confidence and dependence upon his guard, without trusting to his avoiding an attack of an opponent by turning or drawing back the body to escape from it.

In delivering a thrust, very little force is necessary, when the horse is in a quick motion, as the extension of the arm, with a good direction of the point, will be fully sufficient; nor should a cut, under the same circumstances, be given too strong, as in both cases the impetus of the horse will give the effective force, or in the latter, the drawing of the edge can very frequently be applied with advantage, particularly when the point may not have taken effect, when, by a quick turn of the wrist, the edge is drawn along the face of your opponent, or any part which more immediately comes in contact with it.

A similar advantage may be gained after forming a guard, particularly the second, with the point of the sword kept well forward. The forcing also of the edge can be resorted to, when very near and closely pressed upon by an adversary, by suddenly extending the arm, and directing the edge across the face, or where the opening is shown: in this case, however, the hand should not be carried more than absolutely requisite either to the right or left, so as not by too wide a movement, to offer an equal chance to your opponent.

Where sufficient space of ground allows of choosing the point of attack, you should endeavour to turn this to your own advantage, if not, at all events to avoid its being made on your left rear; when change of position will bring you upon an equality with your opponent, either by making a sudden halt, so as to allow him to pass, then pressing upon his left rear, or by turning quickly to the left-about, and thereby having your right also opposed to his. Should you be prevented from doing this, and he still keep upon your left, you must bear up as close as possible to him, otherwise your opposition will be ineffectual; for in his situation, by keeping at the proper distance from you, his cut will reach, when yours cannot, and consequently you are reduced to the defensive alone.

In meeting an opponent on the Left front, turn sharply to the left on your own ground, which brings you immediately with your sword-arm free, and at liberty to act upon his left; and in meeting him upon the right-front, press his horse quickly on, by a sharp turn to the right, gain his left rear, or, if pursued, endeavour to keep your adversary on the right rear, when the distance will be always in your favour, and you may by the rear cut (sixth, by turning the body well to the right rear) and point, keep checking his advance with impunity. When attacked by more than one, you will naturally endeavour to keep them either on the right or left; but when they have been enabled to place themselves on both sides, press close upon the left opponent, and keep the right one at a distance.

Although a regular mode is laid down for drawing the sword, yet occasional practice should be given both on foot and horseback, to come to the guard immediately, and at any required point, without going through the parade motions, &c, which will prepare the swordsman for any sudden attack of an enemy.

The defence or attack against the lance, must depend greatly upon the rider: for, admitting that the lancer is equally well mounted, and skilful in the management of his horse, he will always endeavour to keep at such a distance as to be out of your reach, while he can easily make good his thrust, from the greater length of the lance than that of the sword; and he will very frequently succeed in directing his point at your horse, which, becoming unruly from the pain of a wound, will leave you exposed to the attack of your opponent.

You must, therefore, invariably endeavour to gain his right rear, when he is less able to attack or defend, as his position, from its being so contracted, becomes weak; whereas, if he has the advantage of resting his lance upon the bridle-arm, he can lengthen or shorten his thrust with facility and quickness. If engaged on his left, the object must be to keep out of distance of his lance, watching the opportunity to close, either by having previously formed a defence, or by bearing the lance out of the line. In all cases, your horse should be well accustomed to the waving of the lance, without which, no skill of yours, either in the use of the sword, or in that of riding, can be of much service to you.

When opposed to infantry, endeavour to meet an opponent on your right; as every guard parries the point of a sword, so will each defend the point of a bayonet, taking care that the force of your own weapon meets the foible of your opponent's; consequently, it is the bayonet which must be struck; and supposing the attack to be directed, as usual, with the opponent's left shoulder advanced, those guards and parries, which force the point of the bayonet to the front, are, in effect, the most powerful, not from the strength of your mode of defence, but because the bearing acts in such a manner against your opponent as to render him less capable of resisting, or recovering the command of his weapon in time to defend himself or renew the attack.

It gives you an opportunity of following with a cut or thrust; whereas, if you parry to the rear, that advantage is lost, unless you halt, which, of course, affords time to your opponent to take equal advantage of it also. In fact, very little exertion is sufficient to effect a strong parry, if it is made in the direction in which your horse is moving, and from the same cause, all rear parries are weak. Still, however, as security is important, recourse must be had to them when they become requisite.

In defending on your left, a parry to the rear will, for the reason before stated, disorder your opponent's position, more than parrying to the front; and every following cut or thrust must be instantaneous, as, though for the moment you may be able to oppose a bayonet, yet, from your opponent's having the advantage of both hands in the management of it, he may, if confident, guard sufficiently to enable him to fix his point. In advancing against infantry, the right guard, hand high, leads well to the attack, and is ready for defence, or to take advantage of any opening. The instructors should, as much as possible, in their progressive directions to the recruit, impress upon his mind such occasional observations as become most applicable.

Opportunities of thus explaining may often be taken during

the pauses of rest, as no squad should be kept too long either in positions or movements; and when any recruits are more deficient than the rest, the whole should be made to cease for the moment, and only those who are wrong be required to correct their error.

Section 6

Balance Practice and Extension Motions for Infantry.

First Position in Three Motions.

One.—Move the hands "smartly to the rear, the left grasping the right arm just above the elbow, and the right supporting the left arm under the elbow.

Two.—Make a half face to the left, turning on the heels, so that the back of the left touches the inside of the right heel; the head retaining its position to the front.

Three.—Bring the right heel in the hollow of the left foot— the right foot pointing to the front; shoulders square to the left, and the weight of the body resting on the left leg.

Second Position in Two Motions.

One.—Bend the knees gradually, keeping them as much apart as possible, without raising the heels or changing the erect position of the body.

Two.—Step out smartly with the right foot about 18 inches in a line with the left heel; the weight of the body remaining on the left leg.

Balance Motions.

One.—Move the right foot about 8 inches to the rear of the left heel, the toe lightly touching the ground, with the heel perpendicular to it, forcing the knees well apart.

Two.—Raise the body gradually by the extension of the left leg.

Three.—Bend the left knee, resuming the position made previous to the second motion.

Four.—Advance the right leg, and with a smart beat of the

foot resume the "*second position*" from which the balance motions commenced, at "*first position*"—extending both knees, draw the right heel up to the left.

THIRD POSITION IN TWO MOTIONS.

One.—Incline the right side to the front, so that the shoulder and knee are perpendicular to the point of the foot.

Two.—Step out smartly to the front, about 36 inches, with the knees in a perpendicular position to the instep; the left knee and foot kept straight and firm, the heels in a line, the body upright, the shoulders square to the left.

Second Extension Motion. One.—Bring the arms to the front of the body, with the hands closed, and the knuckles uppermost, touching each other below the lower button of the waistcoat; raise them gradually until the wrists, by bearing inward, touch the breast; the elbows being kept up, then by forcing back the shoulders, the hands will be drawn apart, and the motion is completed by sinking the elbows, and smartly extending the fingers in a diagonal line, with the right wrist as high as the head, the shoulders kept down, and the thumb inclined to the right. For beginners, this motion must be divided by giving the word "*Prepare*" the first part; and remaining perfectly steady, when the hands are brought to the breast, ready to separate; then give the word "*One*" for the motion to be completed.

Two.—Close the right hand, and draw it to the shoulder, at the same time inclining the body forward, until the right elbow rests on the point of the knee, the left arm raising gradually and remaining extended as the body advances, so as to bring the wrist as high as the head, which must be well kept up.

Three.—Come to the "Third Position."

First Balance Motion.—Spring up to the position, as shown in the "First Balance Motion." Three.—Step out to the "Third Position."

First Balance Motion.—Spring up as before.

Two.—Step out to the "Second Position."

Single Attack.—Raise the foot and strike smartly on the ground.

Double Attack.—Raise the right foot and beat it as before twice on the ground, first with the heel, then with the flat of the foot.

Advance.—Move the right foot forward about 6 inches, and place it smartly on the ground; then bring up the left foot lightly about the same distance.

Single Attack.—As before.

Retire.—Move the left foot lightly to the rear about 6 inches, the whole weight and balance of the body still continuing to rest upon it; then move the right foot back the same distance, and place it smartly on the ground.

Double Attack.—As before.

Front.—Draw back the right foot, and resume the position of "Attention."

The object of the spreading positions and movements is to give a free and active use of the limbs, preparatory to using the sword. The instructor should prove the firmness of the position, by bearing equally and firmly on the shoulders of the recruit during the changes in forming the "Second Position" and "Balance Motions;" and when in the "First" of the "Second Extension Motions," by taking hold of his right wrist with both hands, and bearing upon it in the direction of the left leg, in the line of which the right arm should be, if properly placed.

Three.—Raise the upper part of the body, drawing in the elbow, and, when nearly upright, extend the right arm smartly, and open the hand, thereby resuming the position formed by the "First Motion."

Four.—Raise the body by extending the right leg.

Five.—Bend the right knee and advance the body, so as to resume the position in the "First Motion."

First Position,—Spring up with the arms to the rear, and the heel close to the left, which forms the "*First Position*" as before described.

Front.—Come smartly to the position of "*Attention*" bringing the hands and feet, in one motion, to their proper places.

In the foregoing instructions the positions and movements, preparatory to using the sword, have been explained, giving a separate word of command for each motion respectively. The same positions may now be gone through, naming only the word of command the position or movement required, and distinguishing it by the numbers "*One*" "*Two*" &c.

It is intended by this to practice the recruit in changing from the different positions readily, and without losing his balance, which will almost invariably rest on the left leg.

POSITION BY NUMBERS.

One.—Raising the arm to the rear, and the right heel to front, come at once to the "First Position."

Two.—Come to the   "Second Position."

Three.   "   "   "Third Position."

Two.   "   "   "Second Position."

One.   "   "   "First Position," and making him also, in each position, move the right toe up and down, without its motion affecting the body. In all positions where both knees are bent, the more they are so, the better, as a greater spring and elasticity will be gained in forming quickly any other motion.

The body must be generally balanced, and rest upon the left leg, by which means greater flexibility is allowed to the right leg in moving forward to gain distances upon an adversary, or *vice versa* in retiring from his reach.

No precise length can be assigned in moving the right leg to the front in the "Third Position," as it depends upon the length of the stride of the person, but should never be beyond what may allow of his return to the "First" or "Second Position" with quickness and perfect facility to himself.

SECTION 7
SWORD EXERCISE FOR INFANTRY
SMALL SWORD CUT AND THRUST.
INTRODUCTORY REMARKS.

The recruit being perfectly instructed in the preparatory movements, may now take the sword, making him acquainted with the strong and weak parts of it; the *"Forte"* (strong) being the half of the blade next the guard; *"Foible"* (weak) the half toward the point. Indeed a knowledge of their distinctions is very material, either in giving or guarding a cut, as much depends on their proper application. From the guard upward, in opposing the blade of an adversary, the strength decreases in proportion as it approaches the point, and *vice versa*, it increases from the point downward. The *"Forte"* ought always to gain the *"Foible"* of the opponent's weapon, and the cuts should be given within 8 inches of the point, that the sword may clear itself. The sword should be held flexible and easy in the hand, but yet sufficiently firm to resist the cut of an adversary, and to give a cut or thrust with proper force and precision. The middle knuckles are to be in the direction of the edge in all cuts and guards; and the grip of the handle should be held by the thumb and fingers around it.

When the attack and defence are perfectly understood by numbers, the tactician may cut, parry and point after that without following the scientific system.

SALUTE, MOUNTED.

When a salute is to be given, the person or officer will invariably be at the position "Carry sword." A salute is performed by raising the hand, by a circular motion, high as, and opposite the chin, with the edge of the blade to the left, then stretching the arm out, and at the same time bringing the point of the blade in a line with the knee and foot, the edge to the right. The salute being made, the sword is recovered by bringing it back smartly to "Carry sword."

SALUTE, INFANTRY.

The same as when mounted, except that the left hand hangs

SWORD EXERCISE.

FIRST POSITION.—Half-face to the left, carrying the left arm in the hollow of the back, the sword resting, as before, in the hollow of the shoulder.

THIRD POSITION.—Lunge out to the third position, which is springing the right foot thirty-six inches to the front; directing the edge of the sword to the left, and spring back to the "first position."

ENGAGE—Second Position.—Spring the right foot out eighteen inches, the sword-arm to the front, the blade elevated, the edge to the left.

Double Engage.—Is performed by each man springing to second position, meeting sword to sword, with the edges to the left, points elevated, preparing to attack.

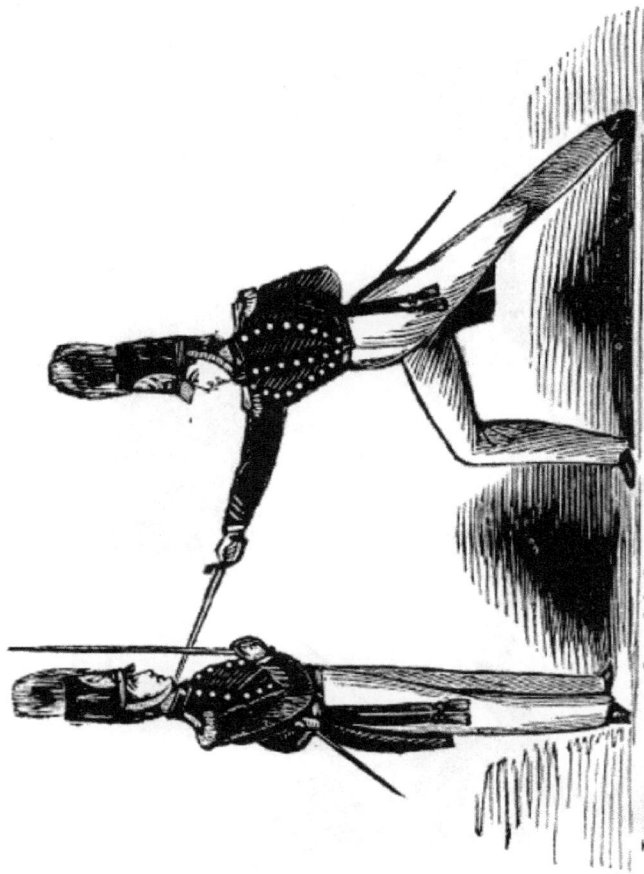

ATTACK.—Lunge out to the third position ; cut at the defendant's left cheek, or left side of his neck.

DEFENCE.—Spring to the first position, form the first guard, defending the left cheek, or neck.

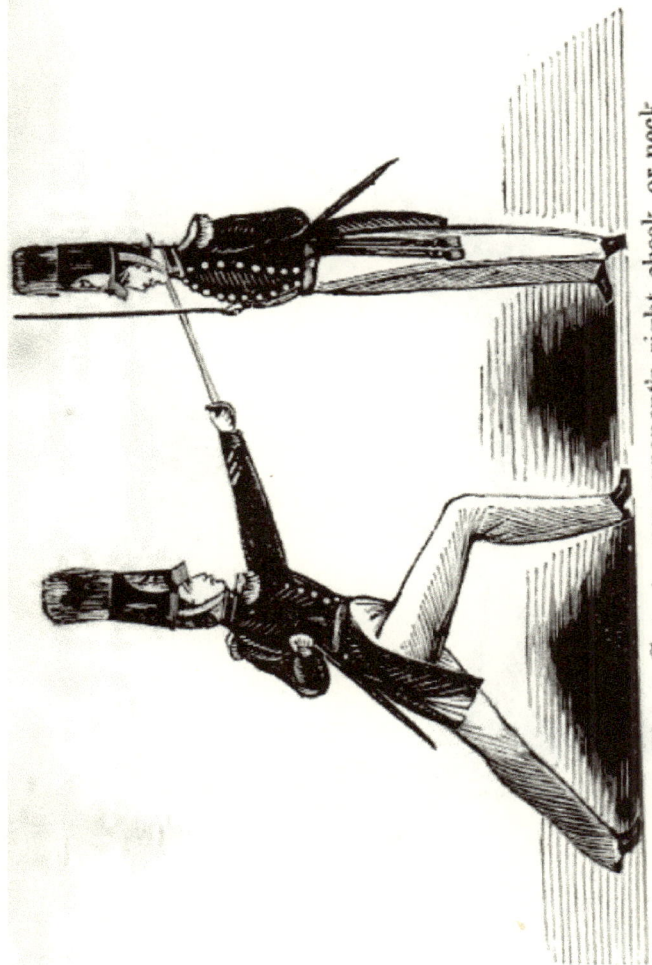

ATTACK—*Cut Two.*—Cut at your opponent's right cheek, or neck.

DEFENCE.—Spring to the first position, form the second guard, defending the right cheek, or neck.

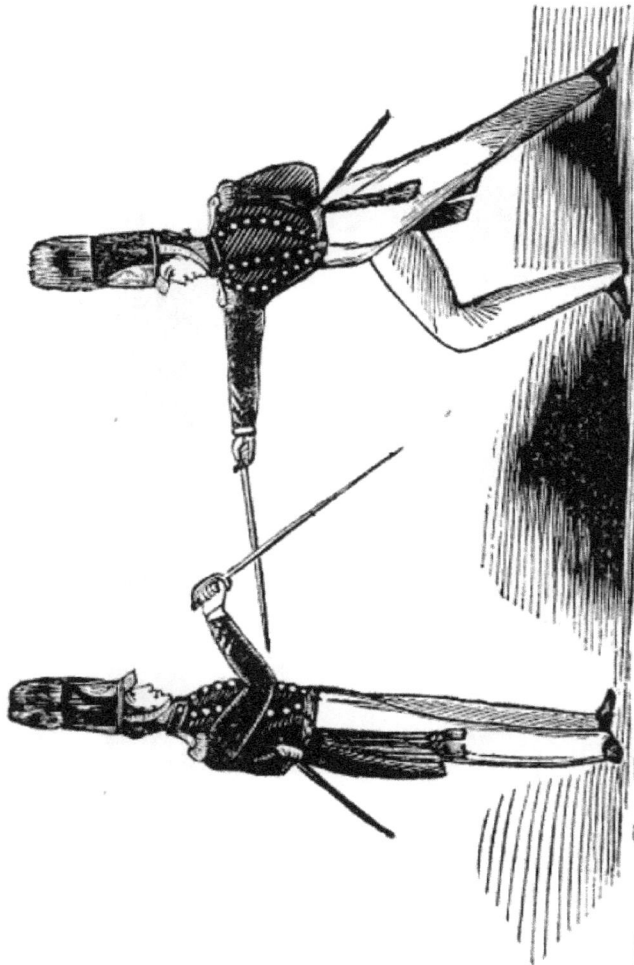

ATTACK—*Cut Three.*—Cut at your opponent's sword-arm, or wrist.

DEFENCE.—Spring to the first position; form the third guard, defending the sword-arm, or right leg.

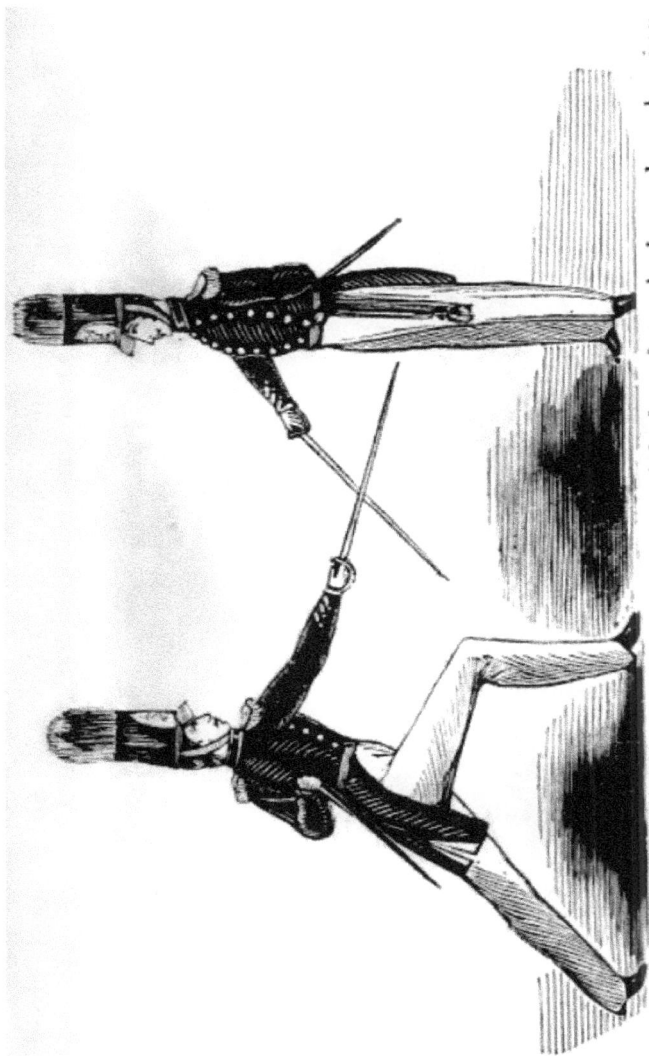

ATTACK—*Cut Four.*—Cut at your opponent's right leg, about the haunch, or bowing part of the leg.

DEFENCE.—Spring to the first position, form the fourth guard, defending the right leg.

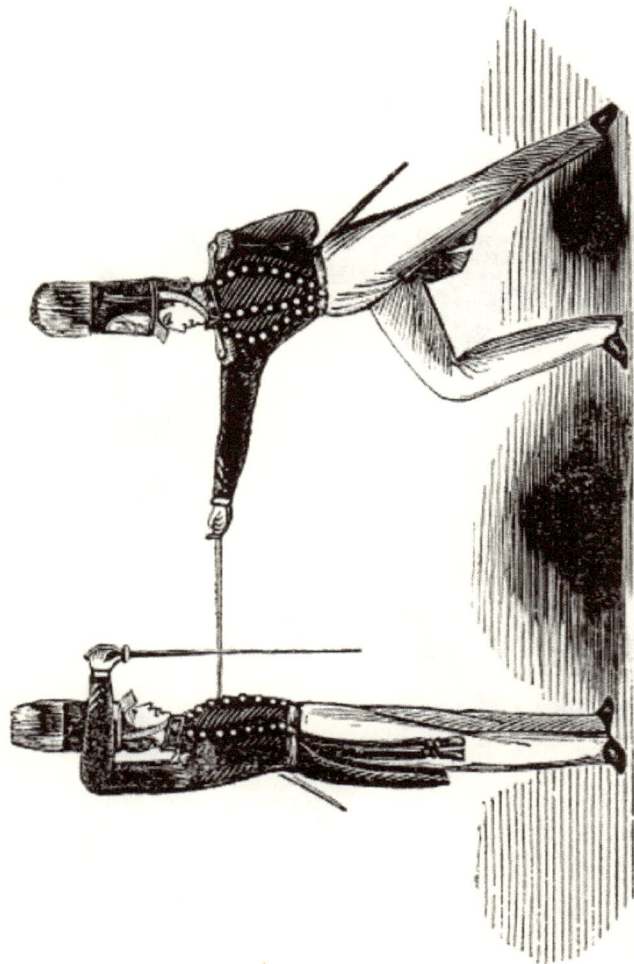

ATTACK—*Cut Five.*—Cut at your opponent's left arm, or side.
DEFENCE.—Spring to the first position, form the fifth guard, defending the left side.

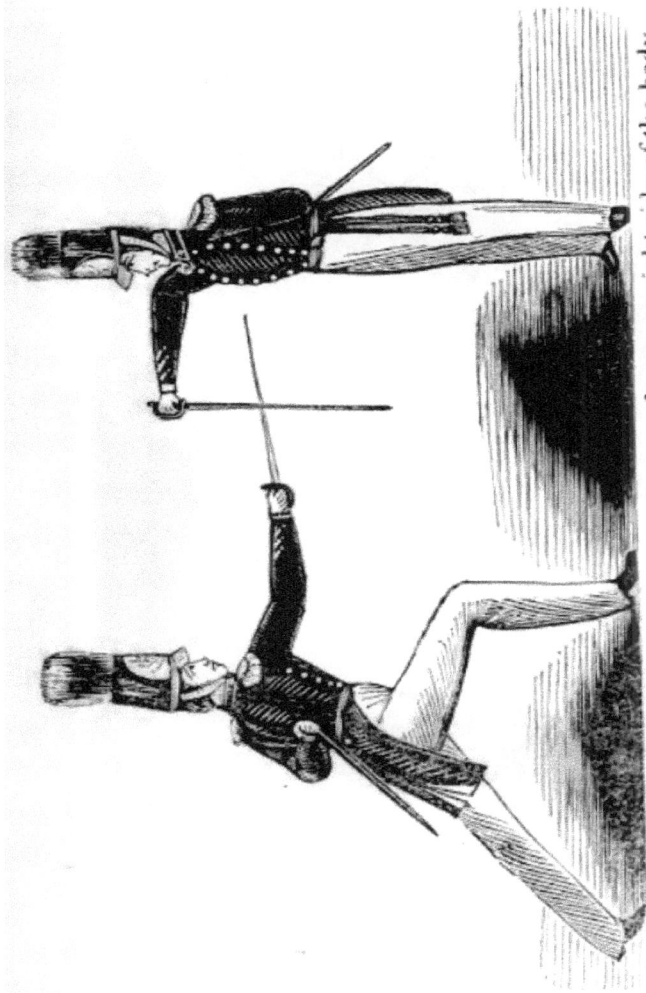

ATTACK—*Cut Six.*—Cut at your opponent's sword-arm, or right side of the body.
DEFENCE.—Spring to the first position ; form the sixth guard, defending the right side, or sword arm.

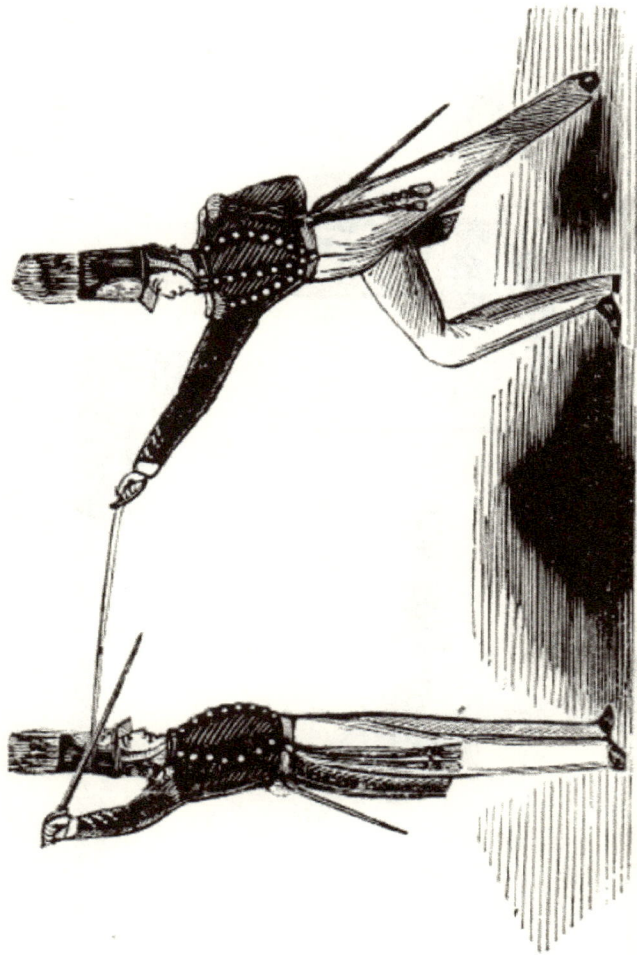

ATTACK—*Cut Seven.*—Cut at your opponent's head.
DEFENCE.—Spring to the first position, form the seventh guard, defending the head.

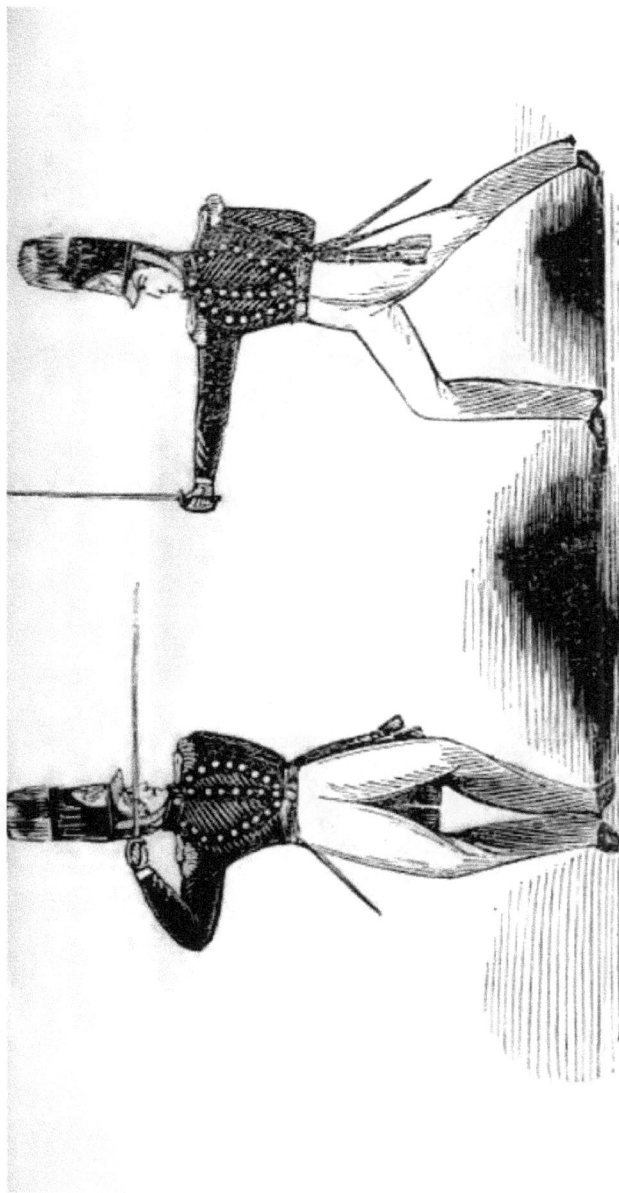

POINTS.—*First Point.*—By standing at the first position, with the back of the hand opposite and against the right cheek, the point of the blade directly front, the edge upward. Point—lounge to the third position, thrusting at your opponent's breast, or front part of his body.

DEFENCE.—Stand at the third position—form a Parry; Parry from right to left with the edge of the blade, the point upward; at the same time spring to your first position, in an attitude to give the Second Point at your opponent.

SECOND POINT.—Place your elbow inside the right hip-bone, the elbow and wrist in a line of direction.

Point.—Lounge out, thrusting at your opponent's body.

DEFENCE.—Stand as before; form the Parry; raise the sword-hand high as the brow—Parry with the back of the sword from left to right; spring to the first position, as before; prepare to give the Third Point.

THIRD POINT.—Place the heel of the hand on the right hip-bone, the edge upward. Point—raise the wrist and lower the point. This point is made at the lower part of the body.

DEFENCE.—Stand as before. Parry the same as the second.

easy, with the palm inward. When the salute is ended, come quickly to "Carry sword."

RETURN SWORD.—TWO MOTIONS.

Position will be at "Carry sword." Carry the sword-hand in the hollow of the left shoulder, the blade perpendicular; capsize the sword over the left shoulder, to the rear—enter the blade into the scabbard six inches; "One," drop the sword; and, at the word "Two," carry the hand to the right side, in a direct line with the seam of the pantaloons.

ATTACK AND DEFENCE ON FOOT, BY RANKS.

The pupil or recruit being now complete in the formation of the "Cuts," and their respective "Guards," may put them in practice according to a regular mode of exercise, as follows:

The whole are drawn up in two, four, or more ranks, so as to be well under the eye of the instructor, with the distance of four paces between both ranks and files. In this formation the whole of the preceding drill may be gone through, either by separate words of command, or with a flugelman; as the following movements of attack and defence, or any part of the exercise, either as front or rear rank files, may be performed without an opponent. Being in two ranks, "Front ranks, right-about face."

PREPARE TO PERFORM THE ATTACK AND DEFENCE.

The files opposite each other, in the first position, with sloped swords. In preparing to perform sword exercise—

PROVE DISTANCE.

The files "Prove distance" standing at the "First position," the point of each sword slightly touching the guard of the other, the hips kept well back, the front rank having their swords uppermost, and the rear rank give way or advance, if requisite, to the proper measure. "Slope swords," as before.

DRAW SWORDS.

Bring the hand smartly across the body to the sword-knot, place it on the wrist, and give the hand a couple of turns inward, in order to make it fast, and at the same time seize the hilt and

130

raise the sword-blade six inches out of the scabbard; by a second motion, extend the arm to the right, the point in an elevated position, edge to the right.

One.—Bring the sword-hand in front of the cheek; sword erect, edge to the left.

Two.—Bring the sword to the carry, by dropping the arm to the hip, elbow and wrist horizontal, sword erect, the edge to the front.

Slope Swords.

Loosen the grasp of the handle, and let the back of the sword fall lightly on the shoulder, the arm remaining in the previous position, but the wrist a little bent upward.

Carry Swords.

By a motion of the wrist and fingers, resume the grasp of the handle so as to bring the blade upright, as before.

Return Swords.

Carry the hilt to the hollow of the left shoulder, keep the blade perpendicular, and the back of the hand to the front; then, by a sharp turn of the wrist, drop the point to the scabbard, turning the edge to the rear.

At the word "One," drop the point of the sword into the scabbard six inches; at the word "Two," loosen the hand from the gripe; at the word three, bring the hand smartly to the right side.

Prepare to Perform Sword Exercise.

Being at the position of "Attention," draw swords, as before stated.

Carry Swords.—Carry swords, as before stated. Slope Swords— As before stated.

Take Distance for Sword Exercise.

Right prove distance. Recover swords; bringing the sword-hand in front of the face, edge to the left, sword erect. "Prove distance." Getting their distance, slope swords, as before.

Raise the sword as before, then by a second motion, step out to the "Third position," and extend the arm well to the front, heads to the right; spring back to your first position. Slope swords, as before.

Engage.—Step to your "Second position," balance yourself well on your left leg, forming an inside guard.

Outside Guard.—Giving a single attack, turning the edge to the right, forming an "Outside guard."

Inside Guard.—As before.

One.—Cut one, directing the edge of the sword to the left front.

Two.—Direct the edge of the sword to the right front.

Three.—Directing the edge of the sword upward, cutting at the wrist.

Four.—Directing the edge of the sword to the right front, cutting low at the haunch of the bowing part of the leg.

Five.—Directing the edge of the sword to the left front; cutting at the opponent's left side of the body.

Six.—Cut horizontal to the right, at the opponent's right side.

Seven.—Cut vertically downward, on the opponent's head or front part.

First Point.—The back of the hand to be raised opposite the right cheek, edge upward, thrusting straight to the front.

Second.—The elbow inside of the hip, the edge of the sword upward, point elevated "Point;" lower the point and raise the sword-hand.

Third.—The heel part of the hand on the hip, the edge upward, the point in an elevated position. When this thrust is given, lower the point and raise the sword-hand.

Parry.—First parry; the hand to be carried to the right, the sword erect; parry from right to left.

Second.—The hand to be raised opposite and above the cheek, the back of the sword to the left; parry from left to right, with a circular motion, downward.

Third.—Same position as the second; parry from right to left, with a circular motion, downward.

Slope Swords.—As before.

The "Cuts" and "Guards" may now be combined; and here it is more particularly intended to practice the pupil or recruit, in showing the guard for each cut, so as to impress it on his recollection.

Guards.—First—At "First position."

Left Cheek.—Defending the "Left cheek."

Second Guard.—Defending the right cheek; the sword-hand to be as high as the right shoulder, the point of the sword opposite and above the left eye, edge up.

Third.—Sword-hand in front of the body, edge to the left, and point downward.

Fourth.—Sword-hand in rear of the hip, the front of the sword being in front of the leg, edge to the right.

Fifth.—Bring the sword-hand opposite and above the left shoulder, point downward, edge to the left.

Sixth.—Carry the hand to the right, the sword-hand to be as high as the brow, the point of the sword to be opposite and above the right knee, the back of the sword to be on a line with the seam of the pants.

Seventh.—Hand to be raised over the head, edge upward, the point to bear over the shoulder, in a sloping position.

CHAPTER 3

Military Equitation

INTRODUCTORY REMARKS.

Military Equitation, the principles of which are the same for all classes of cavalry, consists in the skilful and ready application of the aids by which the rider guides and controls the horse in all his paces, and in a settled balance of the body, which enables him to pre- serve a firm seat in every variety of movement.

The aids in horsemanship are, the motions and proper application of the bridle-hand and legs, to direct and determine the turnings and paces of the horse.

Military Equitation may be divided into three parts:

First.—The complete instruction of the recruit upon a trained horse, from the earliest to the last lessons.

Second.—The training of the horse by skilful and experienced men.

Third.—The practice of the recruit, and remount horse at close files, in the elementary parts of field exercise, to prepare them for instruction in the troop or squadron.

This art is indispensably requisite for the military horseman, in order that, being able to govern his horse by the aid of his legs and bridle-arm, he may have his right hand at full liberty for the use of his weapons, and be capable, on all occasions, whether acting singly or in squadron, of performing with ease his various duties.

With this view, both men and horses should be constantly

134

practiced in the exercise of such lessons as will enable them either to move in a compact body, or to act singly or independently.

The rider, by constant attention, which is called forth in the practice of these lessons, will acquire intelligence and confidence; and the horse, being accustomed to yield to the impulse he receives from the rider, will be rendered supple, active and obedient. The health and condition of men and horses, as well as regard for economy, demand that the greatest care be taken in their instruction and formation; and that their lessons be proportioned to their strength and ability, so as neither to produce over-fatigue or disgust, nor to injure men or horses by too violent exertion.

Section 1
Instruction of the Recruit.

When the Recruits shall have been practiced in the elementary exercise of marching, Facing, &c. on foot, and shall have attained a knowledge of usual military terms and commands, they will commence their lessons in riding.

They may be instructed in small squads of 8 or 10, on trained horses, with stripped saddles and bridoons. The recruits are taught to saddle and bridle for riding drill; and also the proper manner of leading their horses.

Saddling.

The saddle to be placed in the middle of the horse's back, the front of it about the breadth of a hand behind the play of the shoulder.

The blanket, in Light Cavalry, to be well raised into the fork over the withers, by putting the arm under it.

Girth.—To admit a finger between it and the horse's belly.

Surcingle.—To lie flat over, and not tighter than the girth; the upper rings in a line with the edge of the flap.

Breast-plate.—The upper edge of the rosette, or leather, three fingers above the sharp breast-bone; the breadth of the hand between it and the flat of the shoulder.

The bridoon touching the corners of the mouth, but not low enough to wrinkle them.

LEADING THE HORSE.

The reins of the bridoon being taken over the head are to be held with the right hand, the fore-finger between them, near the rings of the bridoon; the ends of the reins in the left hand, which hangs easily behind the thigh.

When leading through a doorway, the soldier placing himself in front of the horse, taking one rein in each hand close to the ring of the bridoon, steps backward, taking care that the horse's hips and appointments clear the posts of the door. When the horse is through, he places himself on the near side as before, after coming to the halt.

Stand at Ease,—Each soldier opposite the near shoulder of the horse, the right passed through the bridoon rein, which has been put over the head, and hangs on the neck.

Attention,—The position of the man, as in Foot Drill, but holding the left bridoon rein near the ring of the bit with the right hand; toes in a line with the horse's forefeet; left hand hanging by the side.

In Front of your Horses.—A full step forward, with the right foot turning to the right-about on the ball of it, taking the bridoon reins in each hand, near the rings of the bit, raising the horse's head to the right of the man's shoulder, and making the horse stand even.

Dress.—When fronting the horse, dress to the left.

Stand to your Horses.—A full step forward, with the right foot to the horse's near side, and face left-about on the ball of the right foot, pointing the same way as the horse at the position of attention.

MOUNTING WITH STIRRUPS, IN FOUR MOTIONS

Prepare to Mount.—*One.*—Face to the right on the left heel, place the right foot opposite the stirrup, parallel to the side of the horse, heels six inches apart; take the bridoon rein, equally divided, in the left hand, and the bit reins in the right hand, placing the little finger of the left between them, place the left hand below the right on the neck of the horse, about 12 inches from the saddle.

Two.—The right hand draws the reins through the left and shortens them, so the left has a light and equal feeling of both reins on the horse's mouth, the right hand remaining over the left.

Three.—The right hand throws the rein to the off side, takes a lock of the mane, brings it through the left hand, and twists it around the left thumb; the left hand closes firmly on the mane and reins; the right hand now quits the mane and lays hold of the left stirrup with the fingers to the rear.

Four.—The left foot is raised and put in the stirrup, as far as the ball of it; the right hand is placed on the cantle, and the left knee against the saddle or surcingle; the left heel is to be drawn back in order to avoid touching the horse's side with the toe.

Mount, (*in Three Motions.*)—

One.—By a spring of the right foot from the instep rise in the stirrup, bring both heels together, knees firm against the saddle, heels drawn back a little, the body erect and partly supported by the right hand.

Two.—The right hand moves from the cantle to the pommel, or off halter, and supports the body, while the right leg passes clear over the horse's quarters to the off side, the right knee closes on the saddle, and the body comes gently into it.

Three.—The left hand quits the mane, and right the holster, the bridle-hand takes its proper position; the right hand drops by the thigh, without stiffness, the back of the hand outward; the right foot taking the stirrup with the help of hand or eye.

Prepare to Dismount, (*in Three Motions.*)—

One.—The right hand takes the rein above the left, the right foot quits the stirrup.

Two.—The right hand holding the rein, the left slides forward upon it, about 12 inches from the saddle, feeling the horse's mouth very lightly.

Three.—The right hand drops the reins to the off side, takes a lock of the mane, brings it through the left hand, and twists it round the thumb, the finger of the left hand closes upon it; the right hand is then placed on the holster; the body erect.

Dismount, (*in Four Motions.*)—

One.—Supporting with the right hand and left foot, the right leg is brought gently, without touching either the horse's hind quarters or saddle, to the near side; the right hand on the cantle to preserve the balance of the body, as in mounting.

Two.—The body is gently lowered until the right toe touches the ground.

Three.—Resting on the right foot the left stirrup is quitted, and the left foot is placed in a line with the horse's hoofs; the hands remain as in the former motion.

Four—Both the hands quit their hold; the soldier faces to the left on the left heel, and brings the body square to the front; as he is turning, the right hand lays hold of the bridoon rein, near the ring of the bit, and raises the horse's head as high as the shoulder.

POSITION ON HORSEBACK.

The body balanced in the middle of the saddle; head upright and square to the front; shoulders well thrown back; chest advanced; upper part of the arms hanging down straight from the shoulder; left elbow bent, &c.; thigh stretched down from the hip; the flat of the thigh well turned inward to the saddle; knees a little bent; legs hanging straight down.

FITTING THE STIRRUP.

The lower edge of the bar to be two finger-breadths above

the upper edge of the heel of the boot for light cavalry, and one inch higher for the heavy cavalry saddles.

FITTING THE BIT.

The bit is to be placed in the horse's mouth so that the mouth-piece be one inch above the lower tusk, and two inches above the corner tooth in mares; the head stall parallel to and behind the cheek-bone; the curb to be laid flat and smooth under the jaw, to admit one finger between it and the jaw-bone, and never tighter or looser, with a view to ease the horse's mouth.

The nose-band beneath the bridoon head-stall, one finger to play between it and the nose.

POSITION OF BRIDLE-HAND WITH THE BIT.

The upper part of the arm hanging down straight from the shoulder, the left elbow lightly touching the hip; the lower part of the arm horizontal; wrist rounded outwards; the back of the hand to the front, the thumb pointing across the body; the hand opposite the centre of the body, and three inches from it; the bridoon-rein, when working with the bit, to be held in the full of the bridle-hand, passing under the long joint of the thumb, and over the long joint of the fore-finger, the top of the thumb firmly closed on the bit reins.

The little finger of the bridle-hand has four lines of action, *viz*:

1. Toward the breast.
2. Toward the right shoulder.
3. Toward the left shoulder.
4. Toward the horse's head.

LEAPING.

For the standing leap, bring the horse up to the bar at an animated walk, halt him with a light hand on his haunches; as he rises, feel the reins only enough to prevent their becoming slack; when the horse springs, yield them entirely; when the hind feet come to the ground, collect the horse again, resuming the usual position, and moving on at the same pace; the body is to be inclined forward as the horse rises, and back as he lights.

For the flying leap, the horse must not be hurried, or allowed to rush, but his head must be kept steadily to the bar, with a light hand. Position the same as in standing leap.

Checking the horse violently, after he has made the leap, must be particularly avoided; as the horse takes it as a punishment, when he ought to be encouraged, and becomes shy of the bar.

The leaping of ditches should also be practiced.

ON THE USE OF THE CARBINE AND PISTOL ON HORSEBACK.

When the recruit has attained a degree of proficiency on foot, the exercise of arms on horseback should form the lessons on drill. As it is necessary for him to acquire such dexterity in the use of his firearms as will enable him to load and discharge them, whilst his horse is in motion, without annoying the animal, or being disturbed in his seat.

It is found that the fire of the carbine to the left, and the pistol to the rear, are the most effective; and that to the right with the carbine, and to the front with the pistol, is the least so.

The fire of the cavalry soldier is never to be had recourse to but in skirmishing; and firing with the carbine to the front is generally to be preferred, because, in that position the horse presents the best mark, and the rider is most covered from the shot of the enemy. The carbine, in most instances of skirmishing, is preferable to the pistol. There are situations, however, where the horseman may find the pistol useful, as when his sword is broken, or his sword-arm partially disabled. If, under these circumstances, he should be compelled to make a precipitate retreat, he may, by presenting his pistol, keep his enemy at bay; although it would seldom be advisable for him to fire until his adversary should close upon him, and the effect of his fire would be nearly certain.

CARBINE EXERCISE ON HORSEBACK.

The squad for instruction is to be formed in a rank, entire, at double open file distance.

Spring Carbine.—Take off the right-hand glove and lock-cover, putting it and the glove into the off holster, or shoe case;

swivel and unstrap the carbine, and seize it with the right hand at the gripe.

Two.—Draw the carbine from the bucket, and, continuing to grasp it in the full hand, bring it to the "Advance," resting the hand upon the thigh, the barrel diagonally across the belly, the muzzle a little elevated, so that it be in line with the horse's left ear.

In this position the carbine is carried by small detachments and advanced parties, when near the enemy, and by videttes on service, being that from which the soldier most readily prepares to fire, and which occasions the least fatigue.

Prime and Load.—Place the carbine in the priming position, that is, in the full of the left hand, at the gripe, (without disturbing the position of the arm, or the pulling of the bridle in the horse's mouth,) keeping the carbine in the same diagonal direction as the "Advance;" place the thumb of the right hand behind the steel or hammer, the elbow a little turned out.

Two.—Open the pan.

Handle Cartridge,—Carry the hand around to the pouch, and take hold of a cartridge.

Two.—Draw out the cartridge and bite off the end.

Prime.—Shake a little powder in the pan.

Two.—With the three last fingers shut it, then seize the small of the butt.

Load.—Raise the carbine with both hands, (without altering the position of either upon it,) clear over the hollow between the holsters and the horse's neck, and carry the butt under the bridle-reins to the near side, (called "Casting About,") letting the carbine turn in both hands till the lock be to the left; then permitting it to slide through the left hand until the muzzle be opposite the right breast, the right hand is brought up to the sight. In this position the carbine will be sustained principally by the swivel.

Two.—Shake the powder into the barrel, and then put in the

paper, or balls, and lay hold of the ramrod with the forefinger and thumb.

Draw Ramrod.—Draw out the ramrod, and put an inch of it into the muzzle.

Ram Down Cartridge.—Ram down the charge.

Two.—Drive it home by two distinct beats of the rod.

Return Ramrod.—Return the ramrod, and hold it between the forefinger and thumb.

Advance Arms.—Raise the carbine up with the left hand, and seize it at the gripe with the right, carry it over the horse's neck and place it at the "Advance;" the bridle hand resumes its position.

Ready.—Place the carbine in the left hand in the priming position; cock; then seize the small of the butt with the right hand.

Front Present.—Raise the carbine to the "Present" with both hands, and place the butt firmly against the hollow of the right shoulder; lean the head in order to take a steady aim. In raising the carbine to the "Present," care must be taken not to disturb the feeling of the bridle in the horse's mouth; and with this view the motions must be made as smoothly and quietly as possible; the body may lean a little forward, and, if necessary, the reins may be a little lengthened.

Fire.—Pull the trigger, still keeping the carbine at the "Present," and the eye fixed on the object.

Prime and Load.—Place the carbine in the priming position, and seize the cock with the forefinger and thumb.

Two.—Half cock the carbine, keeping hold of the cock. The remaining motions as before.

Ready—As before.

Left Present.—Raise the carbine to the present, to the left, with the right hand; and, in order to steady it and ensure a good aim, rest the barrel on the left arm near the elbow, which, for this purpose, is to be raised almost as high as the shoulder.

Fire.—Prime and load as before.

Ready—As before.

Right Present—Turn the body to the right, but without deranging its balance, and raise the Carbine to the Present, with the right hand placing the butt firmly against the hollow of the right shoulder. The bridle hand to preserve its usual place.

Fire—As before.

Shut Pan.—Shut the pan and seize the small of the butt.

Advance Arms—As before.

N. B.—The exercise should next be gone through in quick time.

From the advance the carbine may be carried or slung.

Carry Carbine.—Without altering the position and grasp of the right hand, raise the carbine and place the butt of it in the hollow of the thigh, when previously rested; the muzzle to be carried to the front so as to be in a line clear of the horse's neck, and leaning rather forward, the elbows near the side. In this position the carbine is carried by the advanced guard in marches of parade.

Sling Carbine.—This position is performed by quietly dropping the carbine with the muzzle downward behind the thigh, and leaving it "slung," or suspended by the swivel only.

From being slung, the carbine may be brought at once to any of the foregoing positions, or may be strapped.

Strap Carbine.—Seize the carbine at the gripe, and fix the muzzle in the bucket; then strap and unspring the carbine, and drop the swivel; put on the lock cover and right hand glove, and let both resume their usual position.

PISTOL EXERCISE ON HORSEBACK.

Draw Pistol.—Take off the right hand glove, unbutton the flounce, and push forward the cloak, or draw back the sheepskin and *shabraque*, according to the equipment, and seize the butt of the pistol with the right hand under the left arm.

Two.—Draw the pistol carefully and bring it at once to the position in which the sword is "carried," the muzzle a little to the front, the cock resting in the hollow between the thumb and the hand, the lower fingers relaxed and extended along the butt. This position is called the "Advance."

The commands and motions for priming and loading, are made as directed for the carbine.

Front Present.—From the left hand raise the pistol with the right till the breech be nearly as high, and in a line with the right eye, with the muzzle lowered to the object, the hand lightly grasping the butt, the arm a little bent and without stiffness, in order to keep the pistol steady, and to avoid the shock of a recoil.

Fire.—Prime and load as before.

Ready—As before.

Left Present.—Resting the pistol on the left arm as before directed for the carbine.

Fire.—Prime and load as before.

Right Present.—The pistol is raised, carried to the right and levelled as directed in presenting to the front.

Fire.—Prime and load as before.

Rear Present.—Carry the pistol as far toward the rear as the body turned in that direction will admit; take the aim and hold the pistol in the same manner as directed for presenting to the front.

Fire, &c.—As before, half cock, shut pans, and—

Return Pistol.—Drop the muzzle under the bridle arm, and place the pistol carefully in the holster.

Two.—Bring the right hand to its position by the thigh.

N. B.—Preparatory to firing to the right and left with both carbine and pistol, the position of the horse must be changed one fourth round, so the men will not be in the direction of each other's fire.

CHAPTER 4.

Carbine and Pistol Exercise

SECTION 1.

CARBINE EXERCISES ON FOOT.

As soon as the cavalry recruit shall have been sufficiently instructed in the elementary exercise of marching, facing, &c. he is to be taught the exercise of the carbine on foot, and to be carefully instructed in all the details connected with priming, loading and firing with ball, the whole of which are equally essential to be understood by the cavalry, as by the Infantry soldier.

The exercises of the carbine and pistol on horseback are to be commenced when the recruits shall have made a sufficient progress in horsemanship, as directed in the instructions on Military Equitation.

MANUAL EXERCISE.

The recruit having his carbine slung by the swivel, he is to take it in his right hand near the lock, his little finger touching the feather spring, holding it by his right side at the full extent of the arm, the muzzle elevated, but straight to the front. This position, whether the carbine be slung or not, is called "the Trail."

Advance Arms.—Raise the carbine with the right hand as high as the hip, and seize it with the left at the "gripe ;" that is, with the full hand round the barrel and stock, with the little finger touching the feather spring of the lock; the lock downward; the muzzle raised from the level, but straight from the front; then "unspring" by disengaging the swivel from the carbine, and seize the small of the butt with the right hand.

Two.—Drop the carbine to the position of the "advance," steadying it with the fingers of the left hand; the arm square across the body. At the "advance," the carbine is supported by the right hand against the right side, the three last fingers under the cock, the forefinger under the guard, and the thumb above the guard.

Three.—Bring the left hand to its place on the left side.

Secure Arms.—The thumb of the right hand is placed under the cock; the carbine is raised about two inches, and the muzzle is brought forward from the arm about four inches, at the same time the left hand is brought briskly across the body, and seize the carbine at the "gripe."

Two.—Carry the carbine across the body to the left side, and bring it down under the left arm with the muzzle straight to the front, and about a foot lower than the butt, at the same time withdraw the right hand.

Advance Arms.—Lower the butt and raise the muzzle of the carbine to an upright position against the left side, the right hand across the body lays hold of the small of the butt.

Two.—Carry the carbine to the advance, and steady it with the fingers of the left hand.

Three.—Bring the left hand to its place on the side.

Present Arms.—Raise the carbine from the advance, and seize it with the left, as directed for the first motion of the secure.

Two.—The right hand raises the carbine to the horse, grasping the small of the stock, the left hand quitting its position at the "gripe," is placed above the lock, the fingers circling the stock, the little finger touching the feather spring, and the side of the hand resting on the guard, the point of the thumb as high as and opposite to the left eye, and both elbows close.

Three.—The carbine is brought down to the extent of the right arm, the butt projecting, letting the muzzle fall into the bend of the left, the lock turned a little outward, and the cock raised against the knuckle joints of the first fingers, this and the second finger only resting on the small of the stock, the others shut in the hand, the point of the middle finger of the left hand touching the feather spring, and first finger close to the middle one, the others shut in the hand, the point of the thumb touching the same in the centre of the flap of the trowsers; the right at the same instant drawn back about six inches behind the left heel, both knees straight.

Advance Arms.—Carry the carbine to the advance, steadying it with the fingers of the left hand.

Two.—Bring the left hand to its place by the side.

Port Arms.—At one motion throw the carbine to a diagonal position across the body, the lock to be outward and at the height of the breast, the barrel opposite the left shoulder, the right hand grasps the small of the butt, just below the right breast, the left holds the carbine at the gripe, the thumbs of both hands pointing toward the muzzle.

N. B. In this position the pan is open or shut at one motion, for the purpose of the inspection of the locks, flints, &c.

Advance Arms.—Bring the carbine down from the port to the advance, the left hand steadying it.

Two.—Bring the left hand to its place by the side.

Support Arms.—The right hand is to be brought for- ward and raised, retaining its hold of the carbine as at the advance, the thumb three inches below the bottom of the jacket; the arm to be kept near the body, the guard of the carbine turned a little to the front, and the muzzle to the right rear.

Stand at Ease.—In standing at ease with the arms at the support, the left hand to be brought across the body and laid over the right.

At the word "attention" the left hand is to be quickly brought down, and the carbine dropped at once to the advance.

Spring Carbine.—The carbine is raised from the advance, by

the right hand, as high as the hip, with the lock turned downward and seized by the left at the gripe.

Two.—The carbine is sprung by the right hand, seizing the swivel and securing it through the ring.

Three.—The right hand seizes the carbine at the gripe and drops it down to the "Trail," the left hand quits at the same time.

PLATOON EXERCISES.

The squad being at the advance, will receive the commands and instructions for the platoon exercise.

Prime and Load.—Bring the carbine to the priming position, making a quarter face to the right in this position; the carbine is to rest against the hollow of the right side, the muzzle raised as high as the peak of the helmet or cap, but pointing directly to the front, the left hand across the body, grasping the carbine at the swell, and the thumb of the right hand beside the steel, the elbow a little turned out.

Two.—Open the pan, extending the fingers along the lock plate.

Handle Cartridge.—Carry the hand to the pouch, and take hold of a cartridge.

Two.—Draw it out and bite off the end.

Prime.—Shake some powder into the middle of the pan, but not more than will half fill it; place the last three fingers behind the steel, holding the carbine between the thumb and fingers.

Two.—Shut the pan and seize the small of the butt between the last three fingers and the hand.

Load.—Turn the carbine smartly around to the loading position in which the barrel is turned toward the front, the toe of the butt resting against the outside of the left leg, the muzzle pointed forward and opposite to the middle of the body, the right hand holding the cartridge, is placed against the muzzle covering the sight.

Two.—Shake the powder into the barrel, put in the paper

and the ball, and then take hold of the ramrod with the forefinger and thumb.

Draw Ramrod.—Draw out the ramrod and put it an inch into the barrel with the arm extended.

Ram Down Cartridge.—Push the cartridge to the bottom.

Two.—Strike it twice smartly with the ramrod.

Return Ramrod.—Draw the ramrod out of the barrel and return it into the pipe without loss of time, forcing it well home, then face to the proper front, the forefinger and thumb still holding the head of the ramrod.

Advance Arms.—Throw the carbine across the body at one motion to the advance, and instantly quit the left hand.

Ready.—By a brisk motion bring the carbine at once to the priming position, then quickly place the thumb of the right to the cock, the finger under the guard, cock the carbine, and step back six inches with the right foot.

Present.—Raise the carbine to the "Present," and look steadily along the barrel, place the forefinger before the trigger, but avoid touching it.

Fire.—By the action of the finger alone, and by a gradual but firm pressure pull the trigger, and remain looking along the piece.

Half Cock Arms.—Bring the carbine to the "priming" position, place the thumb on the cock with the fingers underneath the guard, and half cock the carbine.

Shut Pans.—Shut the pan and seize the small of the butt.

Advance Arms.—Bring the carbine to the "Advance" and front, bringing the right foot up to the left.

When the instructor considers the squad sufficiently expert in the exercise in slow time by numbers, he will cause it to be performed in quick time without numbers, by following words of command alone, always coming to the "Advance" after loading, but making ready after the first fire. Prime and load, ready, present, fire.

Care must be taken that the distinct motions are not confused by improper haste.

When a certain number of rounds are to be fired, the caution is given—Fire (—) Rounds, and advance arms.

From the "Present," the firing may be stopped by the words "As you were," on which the finger is carefully withdrawn from before the trigger, and then the carbine is brought down to the priming position.

The carbine may be again presented, or may be half cocked and advanced.

Explanation of the Position for Each Rank in Firing.

Cavalry, when dismounted, is always to be formed in two ranks.

The front rank man, on receiving the word ready, brings his carbine to the "Priming position," and "cocks," stepping back six inches with right foot. After having fired, the right foot is to be brought up square with the left, and the priming and loading proceeded with as before directed.

Ready.—At the "Priming position" as before.

Present.—As before.

Fire.—As before, and when fired, remain looking along the barrel at the object aimed at, until "one, two" may be distinctly told; then proceed to prime and load without loss of time, and make ready.

The rear rank man, on receiving the command "Ready," cocks his carbine, taking a moderate pace to the right, with the right foot only.

Present—As before.

Fire.—As before. Bring the carbine to the priming position with the thumb on the cock and the fingers underneath the guard, preserving the quarter face to the right.

Two.—Half cock the carbine, keeping hold of the cock, then proceed with the priming and loading motions.

Observe.—From the "Present," the squad may be ordered

"As you were," on which command the finger is to be carefully withdrawn from before the trigger. In this position the carbine may be half cocked, the forefinger pressing lightly on the trigger, and lowering the cock till the edge of the flint touches the hammer, then quit the trigger and draw back the cock to the catch of the half cock; also springs may be eased by opening pans and letting the cock down.

When brought to the "Advance," both ranks bring the right foot back to the left.

It being unsafe for the rear rank to fire with short carbines, it may have equal practice in firing by alternate files, as follows: At the command "Right," or "Left Files Ready," the front rank steps out a short pace to the front, followed by the rear rank men, who afterward step a long pace obliquely to the right of their file leaders. After "Present" and "Fire," the word "Advance Arms" is given, on which the rear rank men step a pace obliquely to the rear with the left foot, and both step back into their places with the right; the word "Load" may then be given, and the other files may do the same.

CHAPTER 5

Post Practice

SECTION 1

GENERAL REMARKS.

The recruit, after becoming skilled in the cavalry exercise, should be instructed to thrust and cut at rings, and heads attached to the posts. This practice will give a confidence and precision in the application of the edge and point, as well as the requisite celerity and judgment of time and measure; as each post, having an arm attached to it, to represent a sword, lance, or bayonet, the swordsman is, consequently, forced to turn it out of the line by some mode of defence, before he can make his own offensive movement, both of which must be made with great quickness, and should, therefore, be practiced first at a walk, and so on, progressively, to a canter, &c. The six machine posts may be numbered according to each practice, as the files have regular movements in acting against the heads and rings. The posts are placed in two lines, three posts in each line; they are thirty-six feet apart, with the same distance between the posts.

RIGHT PRACTICE.

First Post.—The recruit is mounted, and at the position of "Slope swords." Advance, carry swords, engage; parry from front to rear the lower arm, and give point through the ring on the upper arm; drop the ring to the rear, and come to "Slope swords."

Second Post.—Carry swords, engage; parry from rear to front the upper arm, and give second point through the ring on the

POST PRACTICE.

First Post.   Second Post.   Third Post.   Fourth Post.   Fifth Post.   Sixth Post.
                                                                           In Right Attack.

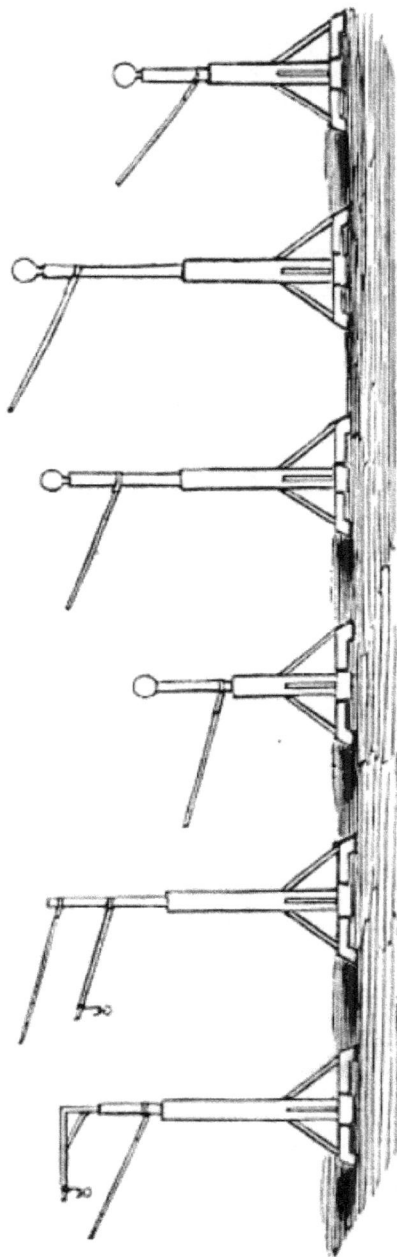

First Post.   Second Post.   Third Post.   Fourth Post.   Fifth Post.   Sixth Post.
                                                                           In Left Attack.

lower-arm, drop the ring, &c., and come to "Slope swords."

Third Post.—Carry swords, engage; parry from front to rear the arm, and give third point at the leather head on the top of the post; slope swords.

Fourth Post.—Carry swords, engage; parry from front to rear the arm, and cut five at the neck, or stick between the head and post; slope swords.

Fifth Post.—Carry swords, engage; make first parry from right to front, and cut six at neck; slope swords.

Sixth Post.—Carry swords, engage; parry from front to rear at infantry, cut three; slope swords.

Left Practice.—Taking the posts in reverse order.

Sixth	Post,	Left Parry	and	Cut Four.
Fifth	"	Second Guard	"	Cut Five.
Fourth	"	First Guard	"	Cut Six.
Third	"	Left Parry	"	First Point.
Second	"	Second Guard	"	First Point.
First	"	First Guard	"	Second Point.

Section 2
Stick Practice.

In the practice with sticks, the same formation is continued as when performing the seven practices of attacks and defence, the squad being extended, and in two ranks; they should then (with sticks and masts) go through the first six at a canter, and afterward both ranks, as in the lesson of the double ride, performing the movements as they pass each other. The opposing files should also circle "Right," within measure, and at a walk, before they are allowed to play loose; strict attention being paid that all movements are made from the hips upward, so as to keep the legs and bridle-arm in their proper position.

The loose play, or independent practice, should first be attempted at a walk, then at a canter; and, that the files may practice on their left as well as on their right, they should frequently be turned about outward or inward. They must also, as in the

154

Practice on Foot, make a slight pause when touched by the file who receives the hit, returning to the position of "Slope swords;" and, although the attack is principally to be directed at the man, yet occasionally it must be given toward the horse, but with caution, so as to avoid touching. For the horse's head, the "Fifth" is the best guard on the near side, and the "Second" and "Fourth" on the off side.

It would be useless to endeavour to state which are the best movements, as that must depend entirely on the judgment and abilities of the parties engaged; but as the loose play should not be allowed until a sufficient competency is attained by the parties, and that they have been thoroughly instructed in the movements of attack and defence, they can never find themselves at a loss, if the science is followed up by sufficient practice, and attention to the instructions they have received.

CHAPTER 6

Directions for Firing a Feu-De-Joie, and Directions for Funeral Ceremony

SECTION 1.

TO FIRE A FEU-DE-JOIE.

The line drawn up at "Order," (double distance,) with advanced arms.

With blank cartridge prime and load, (in quick time;) remain quarter-faced to the right.

Ready.—Carbines to be brought smartly to the "Priming position" and cocked.

Present—Elevate in the air.

Commence Firing on the Right.—The right hand man of the front rank commences the fire, which will run down the front and up the rear, as quick as possible. When the right-hand man of the rear rank has fired, the whole will glance their eyes to the right, to bring the carbine to the priming position; and when loaded they will remain steady, waiting for the word.

Ready—Present.—As before directed. The same to be repeated the third time.

After the third fire, the whole will glance their eyes to the right, to bring carbines to the port together; half-cock arms, shut pans, advance arms, present arms. advance arms, as in the carbine exercise. Three cheers.

Section 2

Directions for Funeral Ceremony

The party appointed for the escort, according to the rank of the deceased, is to be drawn up two deep, with open ranks, facing the place where the corpse is lodged; and when it is brought out, the officer commanding will give the following words of command:

Present Arms,—Reverse Arms.—The right hand strikes the butt of the carbine, which is turned upward, the guard toward the body; it is then placed under the left arm, seizing the cock and hammer with the left forefinger and thumb. The right hand is thrown behind the body, and grasps the carbine; the right heel, at the same time, is brought to its original position.

The officers' swords are reversed under the right arm, the point downward, grasping the hilt with the right hand.

Rear Rank, take close order.—The party will then wheel forward or backward by divisions, or sections, as circumstances may require, and will stand in column, the left in front, until the procession is ready, when the ranks will be open by the word of command

March.—The party moves off in slow time, followed by the music, playing the *Dead March*.

The Corpse.
Pall Bearers of Equal Rank With the Deceased.
Chief Mourners.
Officers, Two and Two,
According to rank, the juniors next to the mourners, or the
body of the deceased.

When the first division of the funeral party arrives near the burial ground, the word of command "Halt" is given, and the officer commanding will order the ranks of the divisions to wheel to the right and left, having been previously told off for that purpose, and facing inward, forming a lane for the corpse to pass through.

Rest upon your Arms, Reversed.—The carbine is quitted by the right hand and brought upright, the muzzle placed upon the toes of the left foot; the left hand, open, is placed upon the butt-end of the carbine, the soldier's head leaning rather forward, the right hand is brought up to the forehead, shading the eyes. The corpse, &c, having passed through the lane, the word "Attention" is given; on which the soldiers raise their heads, and drop their right arms by their sides.

Reverse Arms.—The ranks are then wheeled up, and at "Open order" move in ordinary time, and form in line in the same order, near to and facing the grave. The command will then be given:

Rest upon your Arms, Reversed.—After the performance of the funeral service, the following words of command are given:

Attention—Present Arms—By changing the hand on the butt, raising the carbine and seizing it with the left hand at the swell, turning it over with the right hand, and then holding it in the position of "Presented arms."

Advance Arms.—Prime and load with blank cartridge.

Advance Arms.—Three volleys are then fired in the air. After the third volley, half-cock and shut pans; advance arms; rear rank take close order; return to camp quarters, or barracks, the right in front, quick time.

In marching back the music is not to play until the party is entirely clear of the burying-ground.

CHAPTER 7

Lance Practice

SECTION 1

EXERCISE ON FOOT

In the following instructions, the several motions are explained in terms applicable to the mounted practice; but the whole of the practice is to be taught on foot, before the recruit attempts to perform it on horseback. In the ranks, dismounted, the lancer is to have his lance near the right foot, resting it on the right shoulder, the right hand in front of it.

Shoulder Lance.—The right thumb to slide quickly in rear of the lance, which is to be lifted about half a foot from the ground, sloping a little backward, over the right shoulder.

Carry Lance.—The lance is to rest near the man's foot, the right hand in a line with the shoulder.

DRESSING

Is done as usual, with the only exception that the lance must fall back against the right shoulder, the right hand upon it, in the same position as when the men sit at ease.

MOUNTING WITH THE LANCE.

The horse being placed straight, the soldier holds with his right hand the reins of the bridoon, near the bit, the lance at the "Garry," in the left hand.

Prepare to Mount.—One.—As directed in the system of equitation; but the lance is to be at the balance, grasped with the left hand.

Two.—The man is to take the reins, and a firm part of the mane round the thumb, holding the point of the lance well up, to prevent it touching the men or horses near it in the ranks,

Three,—As usual.

Mount.—One.—As usual.

Two.—The right hand is to slide down under the bridle-hand, the extent of the arm, and to seize the lance.

Three.—The right hand is to bring up the lance to the "Carry," as described in the third motion of "Carry lance," when the lance is to be slung on the left arm.

Prepare to Dismount.—One. The lance is to be raised out of the bucket by the right hand sliding down to the extent of the arm.

Two.—It is brought up as directed in the slinging of the lance.

Three.—The lance is to be brought, in this motion, under the bridle-hand, and seized by it at its balance, the point kept well upward; securing the lance reins and mane well in the left hand.

Dismount.—As usual; but the lance should never touch the ground until the man has quitted the left stirrup, when he is also to quit the mane, and to bring the lance to the "Carry" on the left side.

The lance, in all movements, is to be at the "Carry" or "Trail," except on marches, when it is to be slung on the right or left arm; or when the men sit at ease, then the lance is to rest in the hollow of the left shoulder, the right hand upon it, extended down on the shaft.

Carry Lance.—One.—The lance is to rest with the butt-end in the bucket, on the right stirrup, and to be kept perpendicular by the right hand, which is to be in a line with the shoulder, the thumb in the sling.

The lance is "Trailed" by being carried in the right hand,

at the balance, the hand resting at the hollow of the thigh, the point of the lance diagonally across the horse's neck.

SECTION 2

EXERCISE ON HORSEBACK.

PREPARE TO PERFORM THE LANCE EXERCISE.

This is done in the usual mode of preparing to perform sword exercise.

Prove Distance.—Is done from the front guard.

FIRST DIVISION.

AGAINST CAVALRY.

Guard.—One.—From the carry raise the lance out of the bucket with the right hand, and bring it sharply and securely under the right arm, so that the lance may rest horizontally, the point to the front; its centre balanced in the right hand, which grasps it. The thumb should lie outward, along the shaft of the lance; the arm is at all times to be kept close on the lance, which should rest under the arm, pressed against the body, without stiffness.

Front Parry and Point.—One.—From the front guard the lance is to be moved short and quick to the left, about eighteen inches, over the horse's ears, so as to parry off any point or cut on the front.

Two.—The lance is to be brought short and quick to the right. In all parries the butt-end is to remain firm under the arm, to give it more force against the point, cut or parry of an antagonist.

Three.—The point of the lance is thrown forward by the right hand, with a sharp motion, to the front, the full extent of the right arm, the butt resting firm under the arm; the point is to be given as high as the antagonist's breast, although the body ought, with every point, and particularly with every parry, to give strength and force to the lance, yet the man should, at all times, remain firm and strong in the saddle, which will give force to his weapon.

161

Four.—The lance is to be sharply withdrawn to the "Front guard."

Left Parry and Point.—One.—The lance is brought smartly over the horse's head, the point to be directed horizontally to the man's left side; the man is to turn his body a little to the left, but to remain well and firm in his saddle, only throwing the right shoulder forward.

Two.—The "Parry, left and right," is to be made eighteen inches either way, as described in the

Front Parry.—Three.—The point of the lance is to be thrown smartly out to the left, as far as the right arm will admit, the lance resting on the man's breast, and the right arm close upon it.

Four.—The lance is to be quickly withdrawn to the "Left guard."

Right Parry and Point.—One.—Bring the lance from the left guard smartly over the horse's head to the right side; direct the point of the lance horizontally to the right. Care must here be taken that by turning round the lance it is not raised too high over the horse's head, otherwise the butt-end will strike against the horse's haunches, which will make him fear the lance.

Two.—The "Parry to the Right or Left" is to be quickly made, as already explained.

Three.—The point of the lance is to be thrown out to the right, at the height of the antagonist's breast. The right arm is to be so turned as to pass the lance firmly under it, and support the point of the lance against any parry or cut of the antagonist.

Four.—The lance is to be quickly withdrawn to the "Right guard."

Left Rear Parry and Point.—One.—The lance is to be drawn swiftly round from the right guard, over the horse's head, horizontally, to the left rear of the soldier; the body of the soldier is to turn on the hip in his saddle, as far round to the left as a firm seat will allow.

Two.—The "Parry left and right" to be quickly made.

Three.—The point of the lance is to be thrown out to the left rear of the man, as much as the arm will permit.

Four.—The lance is to be quickly withdrawn to the "Left Rear Guard."

Right Rear Parry and Point.—One.—The lance is to be brought back in a round parry, smartly over the horse's head from the left rear to the right rear; though the man turns as much as possible on his left to the rear, yet he must keep a firm seat in his saddle, or his power of acting offensively will be considerably diminished.

Two—The "Parry" "Right" and "Left" must be quickly made.

Three.—The point to the right rear is to be given, the man keeping his lance close under his arm; he ought to look well back to observe the execution of his lance.

Four.—The lance is to be quickly withdrawn to the right rear guard.

Carry Lance.—One.—The lance is to be dropped with the butt-end in a perpendicular direction into the bucket, or the right stirrup; the right hand as before directed.

Second Division.

Against Infantry.

Guard.—One.—From the carry to the front guard. See first division.

Right Parry and Point.—One.—The lance is to be brought sharply down to the right, in an oblique direction, so as to act against a man dismounted.

Two.—The "Parry" "Right" and "Left", against infantry, is to be quickly made, as already observed.

Three.—The point is to be given firm in an oblique direction downward, the body a little sunk with, and during the point.

Four.—The lance is quickly withdrawn to the right guard against infantry.

Left Parry and Point.—One.—The lance is to be brought from the "Right Guard," against infantry, with a sharp motion over the horse's head, to the left, in an oblique direction downward, as before explained to the right.

Two.—The parries left and right to be made short and quick.

Three.—The point to be given left, against infantry.

Four.—The lance is to be quickly withdrawn to the left guard, against infantry.

Reverse Lance and Point.—One.—The lance is to be carried over the horse's head, and raised twelve inches, then the point turned down, with quick motion of the wrist, and bringing thus the point to the rear; the lance under the right arm; the butt to the front; the right hand, without quitting the lance, is to be shifted while the lance is turned round.

Two.—The butt of the lance is to be carried forward, keeping it close to the shoulder.

Three.—The point is to be darted to the rear, down- ward, in an oblique direction, against infantry; the eyes should at all times, particularly to the rear, accompany the points.

Port Lance and Rear Point.—One.—The lance is to be lowered a little from under the arm, and being again turned over with the butt to the rear, the point is to be thrown from the right, over the horse's head, to the left rear of the man, into the left arm which supports the lance, the back of the right hand upward.

Two.—The right hand slides the full extent of the arm, toward the butt.

Three.—The point to be darted to the rear, as directed in the motion, "Reverse Lance."

Four.—The point to be withdrawn smartly to the "Port Lance."

Carry Lance.—One.—The lance is to be brought quickly over the horse's head to the "Carry."

AGAINST CAVALRY.

Guard.—One.—As before.

Round Parry and Front Point.—One. The lance is to be brought round smartly, three times back and forward over the horse's head, so that the point of the lance forms a half circle, to keep off an enemy's attack.

Two.—The front point is to be given as before directed.

Three.—The lance is to be withdrawn to the "Front Guard."

Round Parry, Port Lance, and Rear Point.—

One.—The "Round Parry," as before directed. The lance is then to rest on the left arm at the port, and to be grasped firmly in the centre with the back of the right hand upward, the point to the rear.

Two.—The hand slides up toward the butt-end of the lance, to the full extent of the arm, keeping the point of the lance horizontally directed to the rear; the right shoulder to be well brought up.

Three.—The point is to be given to the rear, as before directed, only that this point is, against cavalry, directed at the horse's head of the pursuing antagonist.

Four.—The lance is to be withdrawn to the port.

Round Parry, Reverse Lance, and Rear Point.—

One.—From the port the lance is to be again thrown quickly back and forward over the horse's head, three times round, forming a half circle.

Two.—After the third round, the lance is to be brought as before described in the second division, in the "Reverse Lance."

Three.—The rear point is given sharply against cavalry, as before stated.

Four.—The lance is to be quickly withdrawn to the reverse.

St. George.—One.—From the "Reverse Lance," when the

butt is to the front, the lance is to be taken between the fore and middle finger of the right hand; the butt of the lance then to be moved twice, quickly back and forward, over the horse's head; by this motion the right hand gains the power to raise the lance over the head of the man, then to spin it round in a full circle, twice or thrice, the hand to grasp it, the point to the rear; the arm to be extended upward, holding the lance horizontally, the palm of the hand inward.

Guard, and Carry Lance.—One.—The lance is to be turned in the fingers of the right hand, and, after a moment's pause, brought sharply under the right arm to the front guard.

Two.—The lance is to be brought to the carry, as before directed.

First Division.
Against Cavalry.

Words of Command.	Motions.
1st. Guard,	1.
2nd. Front Parry and Point,	4.
3rd. Left Parry and Point,	4.
4th. Right Parry and Point,	4.
5th. Left Rear Parry and Point,	4.
6th. Right Rear Parry and Point,	4.
7th. Carry Lance,	4.

Second Division.
Against Infantry.

1st. Guard.	1.
2nd. Right Parry and Point.	4.
3rd. Left Parry and Point,	4.
4th. Reverse Lance and Rear Point.	4.
5th. Port Lance and Rear Point,	4.
6th. Carry Lance,	4.

Third Division.
Against Cavalry.

1st. Guard,	1.

166

2nd. Round Parry and Front, give Point,   3.

3rd. Round Parry and Port Lance, and Rear Point,   4.

4th. Round Parry, Reverse Lance, and Rear Point,   4.

5th. St. George,   1.

6th. Guard, and Carry Lance.   2.

FOR DRAWING PISTOL

Right Arm Sling Lance.—From the carry let the thumb, which is in the sling, go forward into the sling; the fingers disengaging from the lance and following the thumb through the sling, the lance will fall back behind the right shoulder: the right hand is to rest on the thigh near the hip; the right arm to be held in a natural position, and not forced either way.

Draw Pistol—The lance being slung, the pistol may be drawn and the various firings gone through; great care and patience are necessary for this practice.

Return Pistol.—As usual.

Carry Lance.—The lance to be brought forward by a motion of the right elbow, at which time the right hand reversed is to lay hold of the lance and to slide upward, so as to disengage the right arm out of the sling, and to remain at the carry.

FOR DRAWING SWORD.

Left Arm Sling Lance.—One.—The right arm is to slide down on the lance to the full extent of the arm.

Two.—The right hand is to give a firm jerk, and to throw the lance perpendicularly upward, so that the hand be within half a yard of the butt end of the lance.

Three.—The right hand is to bring the lance over the bridle hand, and to let the lance slide through the hand downward to a vertical position, so that the butt end enters the bucket on the left stirrup.

Four.—Both hands are to be placed near each other, and the right hand to lay quickly hold of the reins; the left hand is to take the lance, so that the thumb be in the sling which it enters, the fingers following into the sling, and thus throwing the lance in rear of the left shoulder.

Five.—The left hand is to resume the reins, the right hand to be placed on the right thigh.

Draw Swords.—After the lance is slung on the left arm the Sword may be used.

Return Swords.—As usual.

Carry Lance.—One.—The left arm is to give a firm jerk to throw it forward; at the same time the hand reversed is to lay hold of the lance, then to slide upward and to disengage the left arm out of the sling; the reins to be in the right hand.

Two.—Both hands are to be brought near each other, the left taking the reins, leaving the lance supported by the thumb of the left hand till the right has quitted the reins, and then quickly slides down on the lance under the bridle to the full extent of the arm.

Three.—The right hand is to bring the lance out of the bucket with a jerk, throwing up the lance in order to bring it clear over the saddle to the right side; the lance is then to slide through the right hand downward into the bucket of the right stirrup, the right hand in a line with the shoulder.

Second Point.—One.—From the guard throw the lance full half a yard or more forward in the right hand without advancing the hand from the guard.

Two.—Give the point as before, and withdraw the lance quickly to its proper balance and guard.

Withdraw Lance.—Supposing the antagonist closed in upon the lancer, by learning to withdraw quickly his lance about half a yard or more, and keeping the lance firm under his arm, he will prevent the antagonist from getting in under his lance; otherwise it would prove fatal to the lancer.

POSITION OF THE LANCE FOR ATTACK IN LINE.

On the advance to attack in line, both ranks have their lances carried till the word "charge," when the front rank brings down the lance to the front guard, ready to meet the object of attack, and the rear rank continues with the lance at the carry, but loosen it from the bucket. At the "halt" the lance is to be brought to the carry. Those men of the front rank who are immediately behind the squadron and troop leaders, must raise the points of their lances when at the "front guard," sufficiently to prevent accident.

ATTACK AND DEFENCE.

To enable the soldier to use his lance to best advantage, in the various ways he may have occasion to defend himself against his antagonist's attack, with the lance or sword, it will be most useful to both men and horses to form them upon a circle, and let the men attack and defend themselves as they feel they have power over their weapons and command over their horses. This manner of attack and defence may be tried both upon the right and left circle with any weapon. Those who are perfect masters of their horses will have a decided advantage over those less so; yet, with so long a weapon as the lance, it requires the horse to be particularly well-broken, and the man to be perfect in the management of his horse and weapons. The lancer at all times should try to keep his antagonist as much as possible in his front, or on his right, and at a distance, as the great advantage of the superior length of the weapon is lost as soon as the antagonist is able to close on him.

This exercise should at first be tried with blunt lances, and sticks with basket handles.

CHAPTER 1

General Instructions

SECTION 1.
FOILS, MASKS, GUARDS OF CARTE AND TIERCE, &C.

FOILS, MASKS, &C.

The foils should be proportioned to the size of those who use them. Thirty-one inches is the medium for men. It is advisable to use a glove on the hand, padded on the back and the outside of the fingers; the masks must have wire fronts stout enough to resist an accidental thrust at the face. An easy dress should be worn, and it is usual, in academies, to have a spot or heart on the left side of the breast of the waistcoat.

HOW TO HOLD THE FOIL.

The hilt must be flat in your hand, so that the two edges are nearly horizontal when you throw yourself upon guard. Your thumb should be stretched along the upper flat part of the hilt within half an inch of the shell, and the pommel should rest under your wrist.

COMMON GUARDS OF CARTE AND TIERCE.

Stand in the first position; that is, your right foot forward with the heel advanced; then throw yourself upon the common guard or carte by advancing your right foot about half a yard from the left. The two heels should be in the same line. Turn your wrist so that the nails may appear upward. Let your hand be on a line with the lower part of your breast, the arm not stretched, but a little bent and the elbow inclined a little to the outside. The point of your foil should be about fifteen degrees elevated, and nearly fixed on a line with the upper part of your adversary's breast. The left arm (which is necessary to balance the body in these movements,) must be raised in a semi-circular manner on a line with the forehead, the hand kept open in an easy manner, the thumb and first finger nearly meeting; your body should be sideways, and your head turned toward the right so as to keep sight of your point.

Let the balance of your body rest upon the left leg; keep the left knee bent and flexible, so that you may incline a little backward; the right knee should also be rather bent and perpendicular to the point where your right foot rests. The position of the guard in tierce is similar to that of carte, only the hand must be a little reversed so that the nails may be half turned downward. The arm should be a little stretched outward, in order to secure or cover the outside, and the point should be as in carte.

Engaging and Disengaging.

Engaging in carte, or in tierce, is opposing your adversary's blade, either inside or outside, when you first join or cross blades on guard. Disengaging is performed by dexterously shifting the point of your foil from one side of your adversary's blade to the other; that is from carte to tierce or *vice-versa*.

The Advance and Retreat.

In order to advance, move the right foot easily forward to the distance of more than a foot, and let the left foot immediately follow at the same distance; these two movements must be performed in the same moment. Keep your body firm and steady, while you repeat this five or six times; and let there be a short pause between every advance. After making five or six advances, observe if the distance and position of your guard be exactly the same as your distance and position were when you commenced. In the retreat, your left foot makes the first movement backward, and your right follows at the same moment.

The Simple Parade of Carte and Tierce.

These are distinguished from all the others, on account of their securing the breast, as upper parades. To perform that of carte, place yourself on the common guard, and throw your hand toward the left, or inward, about six inches from guard, making a gradual turn upward with the wrist, in order to throw off your adversary's blade with the greater ease, at the same time draw your hand a little toward your body, that the opposition may be more powerful; the simple parade of tierce is also performed from the common guard, by throwing and stretching your arm obliquely downward to the right, or outwardly, the nails being reversed by the gradual turn of the wrist, in forming the parade. It parries the simple thrust of carte over the arm and second. The distance of the hand from the common guard should be six inches. The point of your foil, your body and legs, should not deviate from the line of direction, in performing either of these parades.

Section 2
Parades of Octave, Simple Parade, Etc.

The Parades of Octave and Semi-circle.

To perform the octave parallel, raise the hand as high as your chin, the nails must not be twined up so much as in semi-circle; your arm should be well stretched, and thrown outward, the distance of six inches, the wrist should be bent as much as possible, in order that the point may fall on a line with your adversary's flank, making nearly the same angle from guard point as semi-circle. Semi-circle parade is useful against thrusts of low carte, seconde, and the disengage and thrust of carte over the arms. Let your body be steadily inclined upon the left side; drop your point, with the nails upward, so as to form an angle of nearly 45 degrees with the guard point, at the same time stretch your arm well out, raise the hand as high as your mouth, and throw your arm inward the distance of six inches from the line of direction in your common guard, that your point may appear to the eye in looking to your arm.

The Simple Parades of Seconde and Prime.

These two parades are not used so frequently as the preceding four. Seconde is very powerful against the simple thrusts of low carte and seconde. To perform it from carte to tierce, the nails and wrist should be turned downward, the point to be dropped, and the hand opposed outward, as in the parade of octave. The points tract from guard is also nearly the same with the parade in octave, and the inclination of the blade should form the angle of 45 degrees.

Prime is performed with the nails turned downward, the hand raised higher than the mouth, and opposed inward in the same manner as semi-circle. The arm should be drawn well in toward the body, and the wrist bent downward, that the point may fall more than in other low parade.

Section 3

The Extension Lounge, Thrusts of Carte, Carte Over the Arm, and Tierce.

Thrusts are for the most part executed with the lounge, except thrusts of the wrists and thrusts of the extension. They may be performed either after disengaging the point or not. To perform the straight thrust of carte, inside, your point must be directed to your adversary's breast, the arm well raised, and opposed, inside the nails, upward, your body projecting forward, and an extension performed of the right arm and left leg; then push from the thrust, in carte, by lounging out to a distance proportionate with your height. Your left arm should be stretched down by the flank, at the distance of two or three inches, and always raised as you recover upon guard, by way of grace, and balanced to your movements.

Your body should incline a little forward, the head be raised upright, looking outward over the shoulders, so as to have a full view of the point. As you approach your adversary's breast, make a gradual resistance against his foil, inward, by way of cover to your lounge; keep the right knee bent, and in a perpendicular position, with your heel, the left knee and ham stretched, with the foot firmly fixed to the ground.

To recover yourself from the requisite ease, lean with some degree of force on the heels of both feet; the greatest force is first upon the right, then it falls upon the left; by bending the left knee at the same time, and inclining the body backward, you come to guard. The thrust of carte, over the arm, is performed in the same manner as carte inside, by disengaging to tierce, with this difference, that the head is raised upright on the inside, and the hand well opposed, outward, in order to be well covered. The thrust of tierce differs only from carte, over the arm, by reversing the wrist, the hand being well raised and opposed outward.

SECTION 4
LOW CARTE.—VARIATIONS IN PRACTICE.

LOW CARTE, OCTAVE, SECONDE AND PRIME THRUSTS.

Low carte, sometimes called semi-circle thrust, is delivered after forming the parade of semi-circle, in the same manner as simple carte thrust, only the hand and point must be fixed lower. It is an excellent thrust, if your adversary have frequent recourse to his high parades.

Octave thrust is delivered after the parade of octave on the flank or belly, the arm being well opposed outward. If you parry your adversary's thrust by octave, your return will naturally be the thrust of octave; which may, at the same time, touch him with the extension only, without the lounge. The thrust in seconde is delivered after the parade of the tierce; or when engaged by tierce, by dropping your point under your adversary's wrist, with the nails downward; lounge and deliver the thrust on the flank.

Prime is the natural thrust in return, after having parried your adversary's force, when advanced considerably within his measure, and pressing vigorously upon you. It is only an extension of the arm from the opposition of the parade to your adversary's body, the nails being kept downward. The arm should be well raised, and opposed inward.

174

Variations and Lessons on Engaging and Disengaging, Advancing and Retreating, Simple Parades, and Thrusts of Carte and Tierce.

Suppose you are engaged ill carte with an adversary, he retreats, you advance, well covered in carte; he retreats again, you advance with a disengagement to tierce, and so forth, alternately. Take care that you are properly covered on each engagement; his retreat and your advance should be comprehended in the same moment of time; in the same manner you may retreat while he advances.

On the engagement of carte, your adversary delivers a thrust in carte; oppose it by forming your parade in carte, then return the straight thrust thereof. He again thrusts straight in the same manner; also throw it off by forming your parade in carte; deliver in return the thrust of carte, over the arm, by disengaging to tierce. On the engagement in tierce he disengages, and thrusts carte inside; throw it off by your parade in carte, disengage and thrust carte over the arm; he parries and returns in tierce, which you parry by a parade in tierce, and longe home with a straight thrust in tierce.

Section 5
Lessons and Variations.

Lessons and Variations, Low Carte and Octave.

On the engagement of carte, drop your point and deliver the thrust of low carte. On the same engagement, your adversary thrusts straight home, throw it off by parade in carte, then deliver a return of the thrust in low carte. On the same engagement disengage to tierce, and thrust carte over the arm, he opposes it with his parade and returns a disengaged thrust in carte, which throw off with the parade of carte, then with vivacity drop your point and deliver a thrust in low carte. On the same engagement, disengage to tierce and thrust carte over the arm; he opposes it with his parade and returns a disengaged thrust in carte; which throw off with the parade of carte; then, with vivacity, drop your point and deliver a thrust in low carte. On the engagement of tierce, your adversary, by disengaging, attempts to deliver a thrust in low carte, throw it off by performing the parade of octave, then make a quick return of the thrust in octave.

On the engagement of carte; he thrusts low carte, parry it by octave; instantly form your extension; fix your point well to his body, and you may almost make sure of touching him. On the engagement of carte, he disengages to tierce and thrusts; throw it off by your parade of tierce; then reverse your nails upward, and return a thrust in octave. On the same engagement he thrusts low carte; oppose it by forming your parades in semi-circle; then deliver a thrust in octave, by disengaging over his arm, commonly called a counter disengagement.

LESSON AND VARIATIONS IN PRIME AND SECONDE.

On the engagement of tierce your adversary advances within his measure, and delivers a thrust in tierce, or carte, over the arm; oppose his blade by the parade of prime and return a thrust in prime.

On the same engagement, he advances, disengages and forcibly thrusts carte; drop your point and parry it with prime; then disengage over his arm and return a thrust in seconde.

On the engagement of carte, he disengages and thrusts carte over the arm; parry it with simple tierce and return a thrust in tierce; he advances, as you recover, within his measure, forcing upon your blade; form your parade in prime and deliver a quick return of the thrust thereof. On the same engagement, he again disengages and thrusts carte over the arm, which parry with tierce and return the thrust thereof; he forces a thrust, without advancing; parry it with prime, then disengage over the arm and return your thrust in seonde.

SECTION 6
THE SALUTE, ETC.

Place yourself on guard, engage your adversary's blade on the outside, by way of compliment; desire him to thrust first at you; then drop your point by reversing the nails downward with a circular motion; draw your right foot close behind the left, stretching both hams; raise your right arm, and with your left hand take off your hat gracefully; then make a circular motion with your wrist, with the nails upward, while you advance your right foot forward, forming your proper extension. Your adversary makes the same motions, keeping equal time with yours; but instead of forming the extension, he makes a full longe, as if going to thrust carte inside, in order to take his measure, presenting his point at a little distance from your body while you remain uncovered on the extension.

When your adversary recovers his position, after having taken his measure, you also recover, by drawing the right foot or heel of the left; the right hand well stretched and raised, the nails upward, and the point dropped, the left hand raised in a semicircular form, as if on guard, your hat held therein with case and gracefulness, the head upright, and the hams stretched. In this attitude salute first in carte, by forming that parade; then salute in tierce, by forming the parade of tierce; lastly, make a circular motion with the wrist, by dropping your point in tierce, at that moment putting on your hat, and throwing yourself upon the guard of carte.

When it is your turn to push, the salute only differs in one particular from the above, that is, instead of forming the extension, and uncovering the body, you make a full longe from the first position, by placing the right foot or heel close to the heel of the left, and conclude with the other movements.

All these motions should be performed with ease, grace, and without precipitation. After performing the salute, and being engaged in carte, your adversary, agreeably to the compliment offered, pushes at your breast by disengaging nimbly to tierce, and thrusting carte over the arm. Observe that the wrist is never reversed when he disengages; oppose it by forming the parade of tierce; then drop the point, by way of accustoming yourself to make the return in seconde, which may be termed the grace on the parade of tierce. Remain on this grace till your adversary recovers to guard; then join his blade in tierce; he disengages, by thrusting carte inside; throw it off by forming the parade of carte. The grace or ornament to be used after forming this parade, while your adversary is upon the longe, is by allowing the foil to remain flexible in your hand, with the point downward, keeping your hand in the same direction as if covered upon the parade.

Your adversary, after pushing tierce and carte, alternately, commences the salute; and while he is on the extension, you take the measure by longing in carte. Having joined blades in carte, disengage, and thrust carte over the arm. Again he joins your blade in tierce, disengage nimbly, and thrust carte inside.

He opposes in carte; then let the blade and point fly loosely over the hand, having hold of your foil between the thumb and two first fingers, by which you will have a view of your adversary through the angle made thereby. This is the grace upon the longe inside.

CHAPTER 11

More Minute Instructions

SECTION 1
COUNTER PARADE AND DISENGAGEMENTS.

THE COUNTER OR ROUND PARADE IN CARTE AND TIERCE.

The counter parade, in carte, is esteemed one of the most essential, as it baffles a variety of thrusts, throws off the disengagements over the arm, &c. In order to perform it, when your adversary disengages, follow his blade closely, with a small circle, entirely from the motion of the wrist, by which you join his blade always in carte.

If he make a thrust with the disengagement, oppose it by gradually covering yourself with the parade of carte, after having followed his blade round.

The counter, or round parade, in tierce, is performed in a similar manner to the counter parade of carte, only that the course of the point is reversed. For example, your adversary disengages to carte, with a view to thrust carte inside; follow his blade closely, with a small circle made by the motion of the wrist reversed in tierce, stretching your arm, and giving his blade a smart and abrupt throw-off, as you overtake or meet it in tierce.

The course of the point in forming the counter in carte is inward, from left to right, and in the counter parade of tierce the contrary.

COUNTER DISENGAGEMENTS IN OCTAVE AND SEMI-CIRCLE.

The counter disengagements in octave may be performed after your adversary has thrust in seconde, and you have parried by semi-circle; as he recovers, counter disengage and thrust in octave.

To give a further exemplification of the counter disengagement in octave, it is also performed by the first making a feint, as if you intended to thrust octave; he naturally opposes it by forming his parade in octave; then nimbly disengage over his arm to carte inside, and deliver either that thrust, or the thrust of low carte.

The counter disengagement in semi-circle is performed on the engagement of carte, when your adversary accustoms himself to take the parade of semi-circle, by first making a feint as if you meant to thrust low carte, which he attempts to parry with semi-circle, then nimbly disengaging over his arm and delivering your thrust in octave.

THE COUNTER DISENGAGEMENTS IN PRIME AND SECONDE.

The counter disengagement in prime is seldom used in attacks; but being so nearly related to prime parade and thrust, we shall here describe it. It is performed from the engagement of tierce; by forcing on your adversary's blade if he take himself to the parade of prime, then nimbly disengaging over his arm and delivering your thrust in seconde.

The counter disengagement of seconde may be more frequently used; it is performed from the disengagement of carte by dropping your point or making a feint, as if you intended to thrust prime; your adversary opposes it by performing the parade of seconde; then disengage over his arm and deliver your thrust by longing in prime.

SECTION 2
LESSONS AND VARIATIONS ON THE COUNTER PARADES IN CARTE AND TIERCE AND THE COUNTER DISENGAGEMENTS IN OCTAVE, &C.

On the engagement of carte, and thrust carte over the arm your adversary opposes, by forming the counter parade of carte.

Upon recovering, he in return disengages and thrusts carte over the arm, opposes it by counter parade in carte, &c.; disengaging and parrying alternately, always making complete longes with the thrusts, and moving well to guard while forming the counter parades. Make your movements very slow and exact in the beginning, and gradually quicken them. Exercise on the engagement of tierce in the same manner; first by disengaging and thrusting carte inside, which he opposes by forming the counter parade in tierce; in return he disengages and thrusts carte inside, which parry with the counter parade in tierce, &c. thrusting and parrying as above until you quicken your movements with all possible exactness.

On the engagement of tierce, if your adversary thrust octave in low carte, you may parry it with octave, then counter disengage, and deliver a thrust in low carte.

On the same engagement he counter disengages and thrusts low carte, which oppose by your counter parade in octave, and return the thrust thereof. On the same engagement he again counter disengages and thrusts low carte, which you may baffle by first forming the parade of octave, then forming the parade of semi-circle quickly after the other, and as he recovers counter disengage and thrust octave.

On the engagement of tierce advance within measure, forcing upon your adversary's blade; he betakes himself to the simple parade of prime, counter disengage and thrust seconde. On the same engagement he advances, forces and counter disengages as above; but baffle his thrust in seconde by the counter parade in prime, and return the thrust thereof. On the same engagement he counter disengages, following his blade by the counter parade in prime. If he attempt to double or disengage, again stop him by forming your simple parade of seconde.

On the engagement of carte, counter disengage when your adversary drops in seconde, and thrust in prime.

On the same engagement he counter disengages when you drop to seconde; oppose it by your parade of seconde, then return a straight thrust in seconde.

Or if, on the same engagement, he makes a straight thrust in seconde, you may parry it with semi-circle and return low carte thrust. On the same engagement he counter disengages, answer his movements by forming the simple parades of seconde and prime; then counter disengage as he recovers, and deliver a thrust in seconde.

SECTION 3
FEINTS, CUTS, THRUSTS, &C.

FEINTS.

Feints are used to oblige your adversary to give you opening. The simple feint, one, two, is performed by two separate disengagements, either on the engagement of carte or tierce, when your adversary throws his simple parades.

If engaged in carte, disengage closely to tierce, then quickly disengage back to carte and deliver the thrust thereof. On the engagement of tierce, disengage first to carte, then disengage back to tierce, delivering the thrust of carte over the arm.

Feint Seconde, carte over the arm is performed, when engaged in tierce, by dropping your point and reversing the nails as if you meant to thrust seconde; then quickly turn them upward and deliver the thrust of carte over the arm. On the same engagement you may mark feint seconde, and thrust carte inside if there be an opening. Feints, one, two, three, are performed by three separate disengagements, either from the engagement of carte or tierce.

On the engagement of carte, mark feint one, two, as above. If your adversary forms his simple parade of carte, nimbly mark your third disengagement by thrusting carte over the arm. On the engagement of tierce, disengage three times, and deliver your thrust in carte inside.

CUT OVER THE POINT.

This is performed when you perceive your adversary hold his hand low, and his point raised upon guard.

To perform it from carte to tierce, raise your point quickly with the upward motion of your wrist fairly over your adversary's point, without moving your arm from the line of direction, at the same time forming your extension, and deliver your thrust of carte over the arm.

In the same manner you may execute cuts over the point from the engagement of tierce when your adversary holds his point high.

Thrust of the Wrist.

This is performed when you perceive your adversary slow in making a return, after you have longed with a thrust; as on the engagement of carte, suppose you thrust carte over the arm, which your adversary naturally parries, with simple tierce, lean with some degree of force upon his blade, and as you recover to guard, deliver him a thrust with the wrist in seconde.

Return on the Extension.

This is performed after your adversary makes a full longe with a thrust which you may parry so powerfully as to throw his arm out of the line of direction, then with all possible quickness extend your arm and deliver him a straight thrust in return, before he has time to recover, if the extension of the arm be not within reach from your complete extension of the leg and arm.

Section 4
Compound Motions.
(All made at the Same Time.)

Fuge.

Parry any upper thrust your adversary may make with simple carte parade, lowering the hand the whole extent of the arm, keeping the foil in a diagonal position, rather to the left of the body; throw forward the right foot about 18 inches, and seize the back of his wrist instantaneously with your left hand.

Subterfuge.

This is performed when your adversary makes an upper thrust. The instant he commences his thrust, extend the left leg directly to the rear, and dropping the body forward, and low as possible, coming to the position of a full longe, extending at the same time, quickly, your right arm; nails up; direct the point against his side or arm-pit; his foil parries above your head. Recover the guard by bringing up the left foot. This is differently taken by dropping the body to a low posture, bending both knees, the planes of the legs at a right-angle with each other; head and right shoulder elevated; the fingers of the left hand resting on the ground in front of the left toes; the right arm extended; nails reversed.

Volt and Demi-Volt.

In order to perform this, the carte engagement must be preserved. Previously to performing this motion, balance the weight of the body equally on both legs, bring the right elbow well back to give force to the thrust. As your adversary makes his longe, contrive to bring your foil to the carte engagement; remove your body entirely out of the plane of the line of direction, by carrying the left foot round, bringing the heels on a line which shall be perpendicular to the line of direction; weight of the body on the left leg; knee little bent; right leg straight; left hand resting on the left hip; direct your point at your adversary's breast.

Demi-Volt,—The same, except the left foot is only carried one half the distance.

Appels, Beats on the Blade, and Glizades.

Appels, Beats, and Glizades, tend to plant you firm upon your guard, to embarrass your adversary, and cause him to give you openings; they may be performed previously to simple thrust, feints, or counter disengagements, &c. An appel, or beat with the foot, is performed either on the engagement of carte or tierce, by suddenly raising and letting fall the right foot, with a beat on the same spot, taking care to balance the body, and keep a good position on guard.

The beat on the blade, is abruptly touching your adversary's blade, so as to startle him, and get openings to thrust. If he resists. the beat, instantaneously disengage and thrust home. If he use a simple parade, mark feint, one, two; or if he use a counter-parade, counter-disengage, or double.

Glizades are slightly gliding your blade along your adversary's, at the same time forming the extension of the arm, or the complete extension, managing and restraining, your body so as to be aware of his thrust, and to make sure of your own. If you be engaged in carte, out of measure, a quick advance with a glizade must infallibly give you some openings, either to mark feints or otherwise.

The Time Thrust.

This thrust is performed when your adversary is dilatory. On attempting to deliver this thrust, cover yourself well by forming a gradual and strong opposition to your adversary's blade; you can be in no danger of exposing yourself to an interchanged thrust, that is, a thrust at the same moment.

Section 5
Lessons and Variations to Feints, Appels, &c.

On the engagement of carte, mark feint one, two, and thrust carte inside. On the engagement of tierce, feint one, two, and thrust carte over the arm. On the engagement of carte, mark a feint over the arm, and thrust low carte. On the same engagement, mark feint over the arm, reverse the wrist, and thrust seconde.

On the engagement of tierce, mark feint seconde, reverse the wrist, and thrust carte over the arm. On the same engagement, mark feint seconde, and thrust carte inside. On the engagement of carte, in attempting the feints one, two, if he baffles it by his counter-parade in carte, counter-disengage, and deliver the thrust of carte over the arm.

On the engagement of carte, suppose your adversary hold his guard low and his point high, make a cut over the point, forming your extension, and thrust carte over the arm. On the engagement of carte, cut over the point; if he use a simple parade, disengage, and thrust carte inside. On the engagement of tierce, if your adversary hold his hand low, and point high, make a cut over the point, and thrust carte inside. On the same engagement, cut over the point twice, then disengage, and thrust carte inside. On the same engagement, cut over the point, then mark feints one, two, and thrust carte inside.

On the engagement of carte, disengage to tierce, and thrust carte over the arm, if your adversary form his simple parade in tierce, and be slow in making a return, deliver him a thrust with the wrist in seconde as you recover. On the engagement of tierce, disengage, and thrust carte inside, or low carte; if he parry it with octave, disengage over his arm as you recover, and deliver him a thrust in low carte. On the engagement of carte, disengage, and thrust seconde; if he parry it with seconde, counter-disengage as you recover, and thrust prime. On the engagement of tierce, force upon his blade, disengage, and thrust low carte, he parrying it with prime; and if slow in making a return, deliver the thrust in seconde with the wrist as you recover.

On the engagement of carte give him some opening; if he mark the feints one, two and thrust, form your counter parade in carte, then deliver him a quick return with the wrist in low carte, by forming the complete extension. On the engagement of tierce in like manner give him some openings; if he marks feints one, two and thrust, form your counter parade in time; and on the extension, deliver him a thrust in seconde. On the engagement of carte, if he execute low feints and thrusts, use the circle parade, and return a straight thrust on the extension before he recovers.

On the engagement of carte, make an appel, or beat with the right foot, at the same time beating abruptly on your adversary's blade, which will give you an opening to thrust carte straight home. On the engagement of tierce make an appel, beat his blade, then disengage and thrust tierce or carte over the arm. On the same engagement make an appel, beat his blade, then disengage and deliver a thrust in carte inside. On the engagement of tierce make your appel, disengage to carte by beating his blade and thrust carte inside.

On the engagement of tierce, perform a glizade along his

blade, with the extension; if he do not cover himself deliver a straight thrust in carte over the arm. On the engagement of carte make a glizade, drop your point, and deliver a thrust in low carte. On the engagement of tierce perform a glizade, drop your point under his wrist and deliver a thrust in octave.

On the engagement of tierce, he disengages to carte, then disengage contrarily, and thrust home carte over the arm. On the engagement of carte, when you find that your adversary holds his hand too low upon guard, and deviates from the guard rules, seize the opening by pushing carte straight home. On the engagement of tierce, having the like opportunity, deliver the thrust of carte over the arm straight home. On the engagement of carte, if your adversary disengages to tierce, that instant disengage entirely (that is to carte,) and push home.

All these lessons should be performed repeatedly, and the pupil should often exercise with another, who has had equal practice, executing all thrusts, feints, counter disengagements, &c, while the other remains upon guard, making use of the necessary parades, &c.; he should then, in turn, perform the practical movements, in order that both may make mutual progress in the art.

Section 6
Salute—Disarming.

The Salute Previous to Assaults.

On the engagement of tierce, make two quick appels, or beats with the right foot, bring it close behind the left, near the shoe-tie, raising and stretching your right arm the nails upward, and the point of your foil dropped, at the same time take off your hat gracefully and hold it in your left hand, stretched down near the flank; then with a circular motion of the wrist, as if forming the counter in tierce, throw your left foot backward to the distance of your common guard, and raising your left hand, make two other appels bring your left foot forward to the former position, that is before the right, near the shoe-tie, at the same time stretching your arm with the nails upward as before, and in that position form gracefully the parades of carte and tierce; make a circular motion with the wrist and advance your right foot with vivacity to your original guard, at the same time covering your head. All the movements in this salute should be performed in a more lively manner than those described in the salute previously to thrusting carte and tierce; observe also that these movements should keep exactly the same time with those of your adversary.

DISARMING.

After parrying your adversary's thrust by simple carte, or the counter in carte, without quitting his blade, lean abruptly thereon, and binding it with yours, reverse your wrist, with the nails downward, as if in seconde, and with the motion thereof, give his blade an abrupt twirl. If this do not disarm him, it will throw his hand and blade out of the line of direction, so that you may effectually fix your point, and deliver him a thrust in seconde.

Also, after parrying by simple tierce, cross his blade before he recovers; make a strong and abrupt circular movement with your wrist, in seconde, without quitting his blade, and it will either disarm, or give you an opening to deliver him a thrust.

Likewise, if he make a longe with the nails reversed, parry the thrust with great force in semi-circle. The feather parade is a sure disarm. Where your adversary makes a thrust in carte over the arm, or tierce, parry, by bending the elbow to a very acute angle, bringing the hand opposite, with the nails near the shoulder; the fail perpendicular; then quickly extending the arm, reversing the nails, make a powerful glizade on his fail.

SECTION 7
PRACTICAL OBSERVATIONS

Assume a bold air and steady position; fix your eyes firmly on those of your adversary, so that he may not penetrate into your designs; and keep your proper distance and measure. It is a most essential point in assaults, exactly to know these; for this purpose, observe the height of your adversary, the length of his foil, &c, and make the necessary allowances accordingly. If he make frequent pranks, disengaging, beating your blade, and otherwise embarrassing you, with a view to get openings, you may seize the occasion to deliver a time-thrust, taking care to cover yourself well by forming a good opposition against his blade. When on the engagement of carte, by way of snare, hold your point higher than usual; if he attempt to make a cut over the point, that instant disengage contrarily, and thrust carte inside, or you may in preference to this, deliver a straight thrust in carte over the arm.

Be not too eager in making your thrusts in return, as by an over eagerness, learners contract a habit of returning their thrust by crooking the arm, which is quite erroneous. Form your parades justly, and accustom yourself, at first, to make straight returns without disengaging. If you intend to return a thrust by disengaging, you should perform it the moment your adversary is recovering; it must proceed from the motion of the wrist, and not by crooking the arm. The distance of your guard should be moderate—two feet is the distance for men; by a wide guard, you keep your adversary at too great a distance, and have not that necessary command of throwing your body back far enough, when he advances and makes a full longe; neither can you retreat, or make returns with the necessary quickness; the lower part of the body is also more exposed than it would be on a proper medium guard.

Never extend yourself too far on the longe, as it impedes your recovering to guard with the necessary quickness.

Always endeavour to recover quickly, and with as much ease as possible, fixing your point to your adversary's body, and forming the most natural parade, in case he should make a quick return. If engaged with an adversary of a shorter stature, attack him on the engagement of tierce, as being more advantageous for a number of feints and thrusts, than the engagement of carte, particularly for the feint seconde over the arm, &c.

If your adversary advance within his measure, and force in a straight thrust carte over the arm, or in tierce, then raise and bend your arm, forming the parade of prime, and quickly return a straight thrust in prime before he recovers; or if you have not an opening sufficient, disengage over his arm, and deliver a thrust in seconde.

When you first enter upon the assault, you may engage your adversary's blade out of measure in carte, as being easier than the other engagements for executing your different movements.

When you engage your adversary's blade, act on the defensive for some time, in order to discover what feints or thrusts he prefers. Vary your parades as much as possible, so that he may not in turn ascertain your own favourites: for, if a good fencer be found to use one parade in preference to another, he may be deceived with much less difficulty than might be imagined, and eventually be touched by a person far less skilful than himself. A learner, therefore, should practice all the parades, and change them continually, or, at least, as often as opportunity occurs. He should endeavour to go from the high to the low parades, from the latter to the former, with the utmost possible agility, until by practice he is enabled to parry almost every thrust.

If you engage the blade in carte, cover your inside a little; and if in tierce, cover your outside, to present straight thrusts in those engagements. When attacking, it is well to disengage dexterously, outside and inside, forming your extension as if you intended to thrust. If this plan do not afford you some openings, it will, at least, in all probability, be the means of discovering your adversary's choice parades. If he use simple parades only, you may easily deceive him by making feints, one, two, or, one two, three. If, on the contrary, he be a skilful fencer, and uses various counter-parades, you must endeavour to embarrass him by appels, beates on the blade, extensions, glizades, counter-disengagements, &c.

www.ingramcontent.com/pod-product-compliance
Lightning Source LLC
Chambersburg PA
CBHW021058090426
42738CB00006B/407